# AFRICAN LEGENDS, MYTHS, AND FOLKTALES FOR READERS THEATRE

# Recent Titles in Teacher Ideas Press Readers Theatre Series

# African Legends, Myths, and Folktales for Readers Theatre

Anthony D. Fredericks

**Illustrated by Bongaman**

Readers Theatre

**Teacher Ideas Press**

An imprint of Libraries Unlimited
Westport, Connecticut • London

**Library of Congress Cataloging-in-Publication Data**

Fredericks, Anthony D.
    African legends, myths, and folktales for readers theatre / Anthony D. Fredericks ;
illustrated by Bongaman.
       p. cm. — (Readers theatre)
    Author Tony Fredericks and illustrator, Bongaman, present readers theatre scripts based on
traditional African folklore. Includes background information for teachers on each African
country, as well as instruction and presentation suggestions, and additional resources for
studies of African folklore. Grades 4–8.
    Includes bibliographical references and index.
    ISBN 978–1–59158–633–3 (alk. paper)
    1. Folklore—Africa—Juvenile drama. 2. Tales—Africa—Juvenile drama. 3. Africa—Juvenile
drama. 4. Children's plays, American. 5. Readers' theater. 6. Drama in education. 7.
Folklore—Africa—Study and teaching (Elementary) —Activity programs. 8. Tales—Africa—
Study and teaching (Elementary) —Activity programs. 9. Africa—Study and teaching
(Elementary)—Activity programs. I. Bongaman, ill. II. Title.
PS3606.R433A69   2008
812'.6—dc22        2007044594

British Library Cataloguing in Publication Data is available.

Library of Congress Catalog Card Number: 2007044594
ISBN: 978-1-59158-633-3

First published in 2008

Libraries Unlimited/Teacher Ideas Press, 88 Post Road West, Westport, CT 06881
A Member of the Greenwood Publishing Group, Inc.
www.lu.com / www.teacherideaspress.com

Printed in the United States of America

The paper used in this book complies with the
Permanent Paper Standard issued by the National
Information Standards Organization (Z39.48–1984).

10  9  8  7  6  5  4  3  2  1

# Contents

## Part IV
## Southern Africa

## Part V
## Western Africa

# Preface

As a children's author I often have the honor of traveling to schools around the country, sharing my books and my passion for writing. Typically, when I visit a school I will present one or more assemblies, conduct several writing workshops, teach writing strategies to select classes or grade levels, and participate in any number of student interviews. Students are often amazed at the time necessary for a book to go from initial idea to bound volume, how books are produced, the number of drafts necessary before a manuscript is ready for the production process (20–30), and the myriad other duties and responsibilities of a children's book author. They are equally interested in the life and times of a "real live author" outside the world of publishing. ("Did you really see red-hot lava when you were in Hawaii?")

Invariably, during the question and answer sessions following the assemblies, children will pose the following: "Where do you get your ideas?" I love that question, simply because it displays an innate curiosity about the creative process and a solid interest in all the dynamics of writing. Invariably, I respond that ideas can be found everywhere: in the books, magazines, and periodicals I read on a regular basis; in the people I talk with in my job, in the schools I visit, in the places I travel to, and the airports I frequent; and in the movies, TV programs, and special videos I watch at home. I always try to make the point that ideas are all around—a writer just has to be prepared to capture them whenever and wherever they occur.

The genesis of this book is a case in point. My wife's best friend (Vicky) has a daughter (Cassie) who spent her junior year in college studying in Cameroon. While there she met a young and talented artist (Cassie was an art history major) by the name of Bongaman. They soon fell in love, and when Cassie returned to the States they maintained their long-distance relationship via phone calls, e-mails, and text messaging. Cassie went back to Cameroon on two other occasions, and plans were made for Bongaman to immigrate to the United States. Eventually, after considerable paperwork, Bongaman was able to come to the United States in January 2007. He and Cassie married and moved to the Washington, D.C., area.

My wife and I were introduced to Bongaman shortly after he arrived in the States. We quickly developed a strong friendship. I would listen intently as Bongaman would tell of his life in a small village in Cameroon, stories about his family, and how he grew up to became a very talented artist. His narratives often reminded me of the tales I share in the storytelling programs I bring to schools—stories about African culture, legends, and folktales.

Immediately after our first conversation with Bongaman, it became very clear to me that a readers theatre book was needed to share the legends and heritage of several African countries. I also knew who I wanted to illustrate the book! I carefully planned my proposal and sent it to my valued and wonderful editor at Teacher Ideas Press, Sharon Coatney. It was submitted to the review committee, and within a short period of time, a contract appeared in the mail. I spent several months in research and additional months in drafting the stories.

Those initial conversations with Bongaman have resulted in the volume you now hold in your hands.

To be able to share the legends of the African continent in concert with a native African artist is a most incredible experience—and certainly a most incredible honor! Bongaman and I have worked hard to bring you and the students with whom you work the culture and traditions of selected countries and selected people. His creative and dynamic art (on the cover and throughout this book), in combination with passionate stories and engaging tales collected from all across Africa, will hope-fully provide your students with valuable insights into the heart and soul of diverse peoples and their timeless tales. I hope that these readers theatre productions and the accompanying artwork will open your students' eyes to the wealth of information to be gleaned from the tales and legends of a most amazing continent. Knowing and sharing the stories of a people is a good first step in learning to live in harmony with all peoples.

Bongaman and I wish you great journeys, fantastic discoveries, and incredible learning oppor-tunities.

Tony Fredericks

# Introduction

## THE MAGIC OF STORYTELLING

For me, one of the most incredible educational experiences that can take place in any classroom is the magic of storytelling! To watch the gleam of excitement in students' eyes while sharing a new book, to observe the look of recognition when presenting a familiar tale, or to see kids' faces light up when embellishing a piece of literature or timeless tale are professional "perks" that go far beyond paychecks and long vacations. I suppose part of my belief that storytelling is the quintessential classroom activity lies in the fact that it is an opportunity to bring life, vitality, and substance to the two-dimensional letters and words on a printed page. So, too, is it an interpersonal activity—a "never-fail" way to connect with minds and souls and hearts. After more than 35 years of teaching, I never tire of sharing a story with a group of youngsters; it is part of my raison d'être, as I hope it will be for them.

The magic of storytelling has been a tradition of every culture and civilization since the dawn of language. It binds human beings and celebrates their heritage as no other language art can. It is part and parcel of the human experience, because it underscores the values and experiences we cherish as well as those we seek to share with each other. Nowhere is this more important than in today's classroom. Students, who have been bombarded with visual messages (i.e., television) since birth, still relish and appreciate the power and majesty of a story well told. Even adults, in their hustle and bustle lifestyles, always enjoy the magic of a story or the enchantment of a storyteller. Perhaps it is a natural part of who we are that stories command our attention and help us appreciate the values, ideas, and traditions we hold dear. So, too, should students have those same experiences and those same pleasures.

Storytelling conjures up all sorts of visions and possibilities: faraway lands; magnificent adventures; enchanted princes; beautiful princesses; evil wizards and wicked witches; a few dragons and demons; a couple of castles and cottages; perhaps a mysterious forest or two; and certainly tales of mystery, intrigue, and adventure. These are stories of tradition and timelessness, tales that enchant, mystify, and excite through a marvelous weaving of characters, settings, and plots . . . tales that have stood the test of time. These are stories of our youth, stories of our heritage, and stories that continue to enrapture audiences with their delightful blending of good over evil, patience over greed, and right over might. Our senses are stimulated, our mental images are energized, and our experiences are fortified through the magic of storytelling.

## WHAT IS READERS THEATRE?

Readers theatre is a storytelling device that stimulates the imagination and promotes *all* of the language arts. Simply stated, it is an oral interpretation of a piece of literature read in a dramatic style. In essence, readers theatre is an act of involvement, an opportunity to share, a time to creatively interact with others, and a personal interpretation of what can be or could be. Readers theatre holds the promise of helping children understand and appreciate the richness of language, the interpretation of that language, and how language can be a powerful vehicle for the comprehension and appreciation of different forms of literature. Readers theatre provides numerous opportunities for youngsters to make stories and literature come alive and pulsate with their own unique brand of perception and vision. In so doing, literature becomes personal and reflective—children have a breadth of opportunities to be authentic users of language.

# STUDENTS AS STORYTELLERS

One of the positive consequences of regular storytelling times in the classroom is that children begin to understand that storytelling is a natural act of communication. Witness the excitement of primary level students returning from a trip or holiday vacation as they eagerly share their stories with the teacher or other members of the class. Here, the energy level is at an all-time high as family episodes, shared tales, and personal experiences are shared back and forth. Indeed, youngsters soon learn that we are all storytellers, all with something to share.

When children are provided with regular opportunities in the classroom to become storytellers, they develop a personal stake in the literature shared. They also begin to cultivate personal interpretations of that literature—interpretations that lead to higher levels of appreciation and comprehension. Practicing and performing stories is an involvement endeavor—one that demonstrates and utilizes numerous languaging activities. So, too, do youngsters learn to listen to their classmates and appreciate a variety of presentations.

# WHAT IS THE VALUE OF READERS THEATRE?

I like to think of readers theatre as a way to interpret historical events without the constraints of skills, memorization, or artificial structures (e.g., props, costumes, elaborate staging, etc.). Readers theatre allows children to breathe life and substance into history—an interpretation that is not necessarily right or wrong, since it will be colored by kids' unique perspectives, experiences, and vision. It is, in fact, the reader's interpretation of an event that is intrinsically more valuable than some predetermined and/or preordained "translation" (something that might be found in a teacher's manual or curriculum guide, for example).

With that in mind, I'd like to share with you some of the many values I see in readers theatre:

❖ Readers theatre stimulates curiosity and enthusiasm for legends, folktales, and myths. It allows children to experiences stories in a supportive and nonthreatening format that underscores their active involvement.

❖ Because readers theatre allows children many different interpretations of the same story, it facilitates the development of critical and creative thinking. There is no such thing as a right or wrong interpretation of a story; readers theatre validates that assumption.

❖ Readers theatre focuses on all of the language arts: reading, writing, speaking, and listening. It supports a holistic philosophy of instruction and allows children to become responsible learners, who seek out answers to their own self-initiated inquiries.

❖ Because it is the performance that drives readers theatre, children are given more opportunities to invest themselves and their personalities in the production of a readers theatre. The same story may be subject to several different presentations, depending on the group or the individual youngsters involved. Children learn that readers theatre can be explored in a host of ways and a host of possibilities.

❖ Children are given numerous opportunities to learn about the beliefs of selected cultures. This is particularly true when they are provided with opportunities to design and construct their own readers theatre scripts and have unlimited opportunities to discover the wide variations that can be used with a single piece.

❖ Readers theatre is a participatory event. The characters as well as the audience are all intimately involved in the design, structure, and delivery of the story. Children begin to realize that learning is not a solitary activity, but rather one that can be shared and discussed with others.

❖ Readers theatre is informal and relaxed. It does not require elaborate props, scenery, or costumes. It can be set up in any classroom or library. It does not require large sums of money to "make it happen." And, it can be "put on" in any kind of environment, formal or informal.

❖ Readers theatre stimulates the imagination and the creation of visual images. It has been substantiated that when youngsters are provided with opportunities to create their own mental images, their comprehension and appreciation of a piece of writing will be enhanced considerably. Since only a modicum of formal props and "set up" are required for any readers theatre production, the participants and audience are encouraged to create supplemental "props" in their minds—props that may be more elaborate and exquisite than those found in the most lavish of plays.

❖ Readers theatre enhances the development of cooperative learning strategies. It requires youngsters to work together toward a common goal and supports their efforts in doing so. Readers theatre is not a competitive activity, but rather a cooperative one in which children share, discuss, and band together for the good of the production.

❖ Readers theatre is valuable for non-English-speaking children or nonfluent readers. It provides them with positive models of language usage and interpretation that extend far beyond the "decoding" of printed materials. It allows them to see "language in action" and the various ways in which language can be used.

❖ Teachers and librarians have also discovered that readers theatre is an excellent way in which to enhance the development of communication skills. Voice projection, intonation, inflection, and pronunciation skills are all promoted within and throughout any readers theatre production. Children who need assistance in these areas are provided with a support structure that encourages the development of necessary abilities.

❖ The development and enhancement of self-concept is facilitated through readers theatre. Since children are working in concert with other children in a supportive atmosphere, their self-esteem mushrooms accordingly. Again, the emphasis is on the presentation, not necessarily the performers. As such, youngsters have opportunities to develop levels of self-confidence and self-assurance that would not normally be available in more traditional class productions.

❖ Creative and critical thinking are enhanced through the utilization of readers theatre. Children are active participants in the interpretation and delivery of a story; they develop thinking skills that are divergent rather than convergent, and interpretive skills that are supported rather than directed.

❖ When children are provided with opportunities to write and/or script their own readers theatre, their writing abilities are supported and encouraged. As children become familiar with the design and format of readers theatre scripts, they can begin to use their own creative talents in designing their own scripts and stories.

❖ Readers theatre is fun! Children of all ages have delighted in using readers theatre for many years. It is delightful and stimulating, encouraging and fascinating, relevant and personal. Indeed, try as I might, I have not been able to locate a single instance (or group of children) in which (or for whom) readers theatre would not be an appropriate learning activity. It is a strategy filled with a cornucopia of possibilities and promises.

# Presentation Suggestions

It is important to remember that there is no single way to present readers theatre. What follows are some ideas you and the youngsters with whom you work may wish to keep in mind as you put on the productions in this book. Different classes and even different groups of children within the same class will have their own method and mode of presentation; in other words, no two presentations may ever be the same. However, here are some suggestions that will help make any readers theatre performance successful.

## PREPARING SCRIPTS

One of the advantages of using readers theatre in the classroom is the lack of extra work or preparation time necessary to get "up and running." By using the scripts in this book, your preparation time is minimal.

❖ After a script has been selected for presentation, make sufficient copies. A copy of the script should be provided for each actor. In addition, two or three extra copies (one for you and "replacement" copies for scripts that are accidentally damaged or lost) are also a good idea. Copies for the audience are unnecessary and are not suggested.

❖ Each script can be bound between two sheets of colored construction paper or poster board. Bound scripts tend to formalize the presentation a little and lend an air of professionalism to the actors.

❖ Highlight each character's speaking parts with different color highlighter pens. This helps youngsters track their parts without being distracted by the dialogue of others.

## STARTING OUT

Introducing the concept of readers theatre to your students for the first time may be as simple as sharing a script with the entire class and "walking" youngsters through the design and delivery of that script.

❖ Emphasize that a readers theatre performance does not require any memorization of the script. It's the interpretation and performance that count.

❖ You may wish to read through an entire script aloud, taking on the various roles. Let students know how easy and comfortable this process is.

❖ Encourage selected volunteers to read assigned parts of a sample script to the entire class. Readers should stand or sit in a circle so that other classmates can observe them.

❖ Provide opportunities for additional re-readings using other volunteers. Plan time to discuss the ease of presentation and the different interpretations offered by different readers.

❖ Readers should have an opportunity to practice their script before presenting it to an audience. Take some time to discuss voice intonation, facial gestures, body movements, and other features that could be used to enhance the presentation.

From *African Legends, Myths, and Folktales for Readers Theatre* by Anthony D. Fredericks. Westport, CT: Teacher Ideas Press. Copyright © 2008.

❖ Allow children the opportunity to suggest their own modifications, adaptations, or interpretations of the script. They will undoubtedly be "in tune" with the interests and perceptions of their peers and can offer some distinctive and personal interpretations.

❖ Encourage students to select nonstereotypical roles in any readers theatre script. For example, boys can take on female roles and girls can take on male roles, the smallest person in the class can take on the role of a giant, or a shy student can take on the role of a boastful, bragging character. Provide sufficient opportunities for students to expand and extend their appreciation of readers theatre through a variety of "out of character" roles.

# STAGING

Staging involves the physical location of the readers as well as any necessary movements. Unlike in a more formal play, the movements are often minimal. The emphasis is more on presentation and less on action.

❖ For most presentations, readers will stand or sit on stools or chairs. The physical location of each reader has been indicated for each of the scripts in this book.

❖ The position of each reader is determined by "power of character." This means that the main character is downstage center (in the middle front of the staging area) and the lesser characters are stage right, stage left, or farther upstage (toward the rear of the staging area).

❖ If there are many characters in the presentation, it may be advantageous to have characters in the rear (upstage) standing while those in the front (downstage) are placed on stools or chairs. This ensures that the audience will both see and hear each actor.

❖ Usually all of the characters will be on stage throughout the duration of the presentation. For most presentations it is not necessary to have characters enter and exit the presentation. If you place the characters on stools, they can face the audience when they are involved in a particular scene and then turn around whenever they are not involved in a scene.

❖ You may wish to make simple hand-lettered signs with the name of each character. Loop a piece of string or yarn through each sign and hang it around the neck of each respective character. That way, the audience will know the identity of each character throughout the presentation.

❖ Slightly more formalized presentations will have various characters entering and exiting at various times throughout the presentation. These directions are indicated in the scripts in this book.

❖ Each reader will have her or his own copy of the script in a paper cover (see above). If possible, use a music stand for each reader's script (this allows readers to use their hands for dramatic interpretation as necessary).

❖ Several presentations have one or more narrators to set up the story. The narrators serve to establish the place and time of the story for the audience so that the characters can "jump into" their parts from the beginning of the story. Typically, the narrators are separated from the other "actors" and can be identified by a simple sign.

❖ As students become more comfortable with readers theatre, invite them to suggest alternative positions for characters in a script. The placements indicated in these scripts are only suggestions; students may want to experiment with various staging possibilities. This is a worthwhile cooperative activity and demonstrates the variety of interpretations possible for any single script.

# PROPS

Two of the positive features of readers theatre are its ease of preparation and its ease of presentation. Informality is a hallmark of any readers theatre script.

❖ Much of the setting for a story should take place in the audience's mind. Elaborate scenery is not necessary—simple props are often the best. For example:

  – A branch or potted plant can serve as a tree.

  – A drawing on the chalkboard can illustrate a village.

  – A hand-lettered sign can designate one part of the staging area as a particular scene (e.g., field, forest).

  – A sheet of aluminum foil or a remnant of blue cloth can be used to simulate a lake or pond.

❖ Costumes for the actors are unnecessary. A few simple items may be suggested by students. For example:

  – Hats or scarves can be used by major characters.

  – A paper cutout can serve as a bow and arrow or other weapon.

  – Old clothing (borrowed from parents) can be used as warranted.

❖ Some teachers and librarians have discovered that the addition of appropriate music or sound effects can enhance a readers theatre presentation. For example, the roaring of a lion or the braying of a zebra may be used in the background for animal tales. The chattering of monkeys can be played as sound effects in a tale about monkeys. African tribal music can serve as a backdrop to many of these readers theatre productions.

❖ It's important to remember that the emphasis in readers theatre is on the reading, not on any accompanying "features." The best presentations are often the simplest.

# DELIVERY

I've often found it advantageous to let students know that the only difference between a readers theatre presentation and a movie role is that they will have a script in their hands. This allows them to focus more on *presenting* rather than *memorizing* a script.

❖ When first introduced to readers theatre, students often have a tendency to "read into" their scripts. Encourage students to look up from their scripts and interact with other characters or the audience as necessary.

❖ Practicing the script beforehand can eliminate the problem of students burying their heads in the pages. Children come to understand the need to involve the audience as much as possible in the development of the story.

❖ Voice projection and delivery are important in allowing the audience to understand character actions. The proper mood and intent need to be established, which is possible when children are familiar and comfortable with each character's "style."

❖ Children should *not* memorize their lines, but rather should rehearse them sufficiently so that they are "comfortable" with them. Again, the emphasis is on delivery, so be sure to suggest different types of voice (e.g., angry, irritated, calm, frustrated, excited) that children may wish to use for their particular character(s).

# POST-PRESENTATION

As a wise author once said, "The play's the thing." So it is with readers theatre. In other words, the mere act of presenting a readers theatre script is complete in and of itself. It is not necessary, or even required, to do any type of formalized evaluation after readers theatre. Once again, the emphasis is on informality. Readers theatre should and can be a pleasurable and stimulating experience for children.

What follows are a few ideas you may want to share with students. In doing so, you will be providing youngsters with important languaging opportunities that extend and promote all aspects of your social studies or language arts program.

❖ Invite students to suggest other characters who could be added to the script.

❖ Invite students to suggest new or alternate dialogue for various characters

❖ Invite students to suggest new or different setting(s) for the script.

❖ Invite students to talk about their reactions to various characters' expressions, tone of voice, presentations, or dialogues.

❖ After a presentation, invite youngsters to suggest any modifications or changes needed in the script.

❖ Invite the "cast" members to maintain "production logs" or reading response logs in which they record their thoughts and perceptions about the presentation. Encourage them to share their logs with other class members.

Presenting a readers theatre script need not be an elaborate or extensive production. As children become more familiar with and polished in using readers theatre, they will be able to suggest a multitude of presentation possibilities for future scripts. It is important to help children assume a measure of self-initiated responsibility in the delivery of any readers theatre. You will be helping to ensure their personal engagement and active participation in this most valuable of language arts activities.

It is hoped that you and your students will find an abundance of readers theatre scripts in this book for use in your own classroom. But these scripts should also serve as an impetus for the discovery of other tales, legends, and myths about the people of Africa. By providing opportunities for your students to begin learning about the cultures of this diverse and spectacular continent, you will be offering them an exciting new educational experience.

# Brief Notes on Selected African Countries

## UGANDA ("Fesito Goes to Market")

Uganda is located in east-central Africa, north and northwest of Lake Victoria. A landlocked country, it is bordered by Sudan on the north, Kenya on the east, Tanzania on the south, Rwanda on the southwest, and Zaire on the northwest. Most of Uganda consists of a plateau about 4,000 feet high. Along its western border are the Ruwenzori Mountains, which reach heights of over 16,000 feet. On the eastern frontier is Mount Elgon, which is 14,178 feet high.

Luganda is the most widely spoken language in Uganda. It is spoken predominantly in and around Kampala, the capital city. The Lusoga and Runyankore languages are the next most common, spoken predominantly in the southeastern and southwestern parts of the country.

## KENYA ("The Lion, the Hare, and the Hyena")

Kenya, on the eastern coast of Africa, lies on the equator. It is bordered on the north by Sudan and Ethiopia, on the east by Somalia, on the southeast by the Indian Ocean, on the southwest by Tanzania, and on the west by Lake Victoria and Uganda. Kenya is noted primarily for its topographical variety. It has low-lying coastal regions contrasted with towering mountain ranges.

Most of the people of Kenya live in the southwest portion of the country, a high plateau that is very fertile and ideal for growing crops. The northern section of Kenya is desertlike and extremely arid. One of the most well-known geographical features of Kenya is the Great African Rift Valley—a valuable archeological area in which remains of early humans have been discovered.

## ZIMBABWE ("Tiyotiyo"; "The Cat Who Came Indoors")

Zimbabwe is a landlocked country in south-central Africa. It lies between the Zambezi River to the north and the Limpopo River to the south. The country borders Mozambique to the north and east, South Africa to the south, Botswana to the southwest, and Zambia to the northwest and north.

Most of Zimbabwe is rolling plateau, with over 75 percent of it lying between 2,000 and 5,000 feet in elevation. This area, known as the high veldt, covers about 400 miles of the country. The highest point in Zimbabwe is Mount Inyangani (8,517 feet). Many rivers crisscross the country, and it is well known for spectacular waterfalls and fast-moving rapids.

From *African Legends, Myths, and Folktales for Readers Theatre* by Anthony D. Fredericks. Westport, CT: Teacher Ideas Press. Copyright © 2008.

# ZAMBIA ("The Hare's Revenge")

Zambia is a landlocked country in Africa. It is located between the southern rim of the Zaire Basin and the Zambezi River. Zambia borders Tanzania to the northeast, Malawi to the east, Mozambique and Zimbabwe to the southeast, Botswana and Namibia to the south, Angola to the west, and Zaire to the northwest.

Most of the land in Zambia is a high plateau, lying between 3,500 and 4,500 feet above sea level. The major river in Zambia is the Zambezi, which is unnavigable due to several major waterfalls and rapids. Three large natural lakes, the Banweulu, Mweru and Tanganyika, are all situated in the northern region.

# TANZANIA ("The Enchanting Song of the Magical Bird")

Located in east Africa, just south of the equator, Tanzania has borders with Uganda and Kenya to the north, Mozambique and Malawi to the south, Zambia to the southwest and Zaire, and Burundi and Rwanda to the west. The greater part of the country is made up of plateau, averaging 3,000 to 4,500 feet in height. On the borders are three large lakes: Victoria, the second-largest freshwater lake in the world; Tanganyika, the second-deepest lake in the world (after Lake Baykal); and Lake Malawi.

The history of Tanzania goes back almost two million years. Many fossils of early humans have been found at Olduvai Gorge by Louis Leakey and Mary Leakey. Artifacts of later Paleolithic cultures have also been found in Tanzania.

# CONGO ("The Boy Who Wanted the Moon")

The Congo is located on the western coastline of central Africa, bordering the southern Atlantic Ocean to the west, Angola to the south, the Democratic Republic of the Congo (formerly Zaire) to the south and east, the Central Africa Republic and Cameroon to the north, and Gabon to the northwest.

The terrain of Congo consists of a narrow, low-lying coastal plain. This plain is primarily grassland and is inhabited by many species of animals. Farther inland are the highlands and the northern region, consisting mainly of equatorial rain forest. Like the plains, the rain forest contains an enormous variety of wildlife.

# CAMEROON ("Monkey and Crocodiles")

Situated in west Africa, Cameroon (the homeland of Bongaman) is shaped like an elongated triangle. It borders Chad to the north and northeast; the Central African Republic to the east; Congo, Gabon and Equatorial Guinea to the south; the Gulf of Guinea (Atlantic Ocean) to the southwest; and Nigeria to the west and northwest.

With more than 200 ethnic groups, Cameroon has one of the most diverse populations in Africa. Bantu-speaking peoples, such as the Douala, predominate along the southern coast and in the forested areas. In the highlands are the Bamiléké. Important northern groups include the Fulani and the Kirdi. English and French are the official languages, but there are also 24 major African language groups throughout the country.

# CENTRAL AFRICAN REPUBLIC ("The Guardian of the Pool")

As the name suggests, the Central African Republic lies in central Africa entirely within the tropical zone. Completely landlocked, it is bordered on the north by Chad, on the east by Sudan, on the south by Zaire and the Congo, and on the west by Cameroon. The land consists of an undulating plateau varying in altitude from 2,000 to 2,500 feet. The country is drained by two river systems: the Ugangi and its tributaries in the south and the tributaries of the Shari and Longone Rivers in the north.

# DEMOCRATIC REPUBLIC OF THE CONGO ("Shansa Mutongo Shima")

The Democratic Republic of the Congo (formerly Zaire) is situated in central Africa and crosses the equator in the north-central region. The third largest country in Africa, it is bordered by the Central African Republic on the north; Sudan on the northeast; Uganda, Rwanda, Burundi and Tanzania on the east; Zambia on the south and southeast; Angola on the west and southwest; and the Congo Republic on the west.

The 2,733-mile-long Congo River is the principal river. The highest altitudes are found along the eastern fringe of the country, on the edge of the Great African Rift Valley. The most notable mountain is Mount Ruwenzori, which rises to a height of 16,795 feet.

# TUNISIA ("The Merchant of Tarbooshes")

Tunisia is located on the northern coast of Africa. The country has boundaries with Algeria to the west, Libya to the southeast, and the Mediterranean Sea to the north and east.

The Atlas Mountains divide the country into two regions, the water-rich north and the semiarid south. The northern region, which contains the Kroumirie Forest, Bizerte, and the Medjerda River Valley, is further divided into three subregions: the northwest, with extensive cork forests; the north-central, with its fertile grasslands, and the northeast from Tunis to Cap Bon, noted for its livestock, citrus fruits, and garden produce.

# ALGERIA ("The Jackal and the Farmer")

Algeria is the second-largest country in Africa (Sudan being the largest) and is situated in northwestern Africa. Its northern coastline runs along the Mediterranean Sea. It is bordered on the east by Tunisia and Libya, on the southeast and south by Niger, on the south and south west by Mali, on the west by Mauritania, and on the west and northwest by Morocco.

The great majority of Algeria's inhabitants are of Arab-Berber descent. Beginning in the late seventh century A.D., the Berbers adopted the Arabic language and Islam from the small number of Arabs who settled in the country. Today Arabic is the main language.

From *African Legends, Myths, and Folktales for Readers Theatre* by Anthony D. Fredericks. Westport, CT: Teacher Ideas Press. Copyright © 2008.

# MOROCCO ("The Clever Snake Charmer")

Situated in the northwestern corner of Africa, Morocco has borders with Algeria to the east and southeast, Mauritania to the south, and the Atlantic Ocean to the west.

The country is divided into three natural regions: the fertile northern coastal plaint along the Mediterranean, which contains the Er Rif, mountains; the rich plateaus and lowlands lying between the rugged Atlas Mountains; and the semiarid area in southern and eastern Morocco, which merges into the Sahara Desert. The Atlas Mountains, with an average elevation of 11,000 feet, contain some of the highest peaks of North Africa, including Mount Toubkal (13,665 feet), the highest of all.

# EGYPT ("A Most Wise Baker")

Situated at the northeastern corner of Africa, Egypt is bordered on the north by the Mediterranean Sea, on the east by Israel and the Red Sea, on the south by Sudan, and on the west by Libya. Egypt is most noted for its spectacular archeological sites, including the pyramids and tombs of the pharaohs.

The bulk of the country is covered by the Sahara Desert. The outstanding geographical feature is the Nile River. Here farmers, for thousands of years, have depended on the annual floods to provide sufficient water necessary for agriculture. The vast majority of Egypt's inhabitants live in the Nile Valley and delta, and the rest of the country (about 96 percent of Egypt's total land area) is sparsely populated.

# BOTSWANA ("The Hare and the Hyena")

Botswana is located in southern Africa. It has land borders with Zimbabwe to the northeast, South Africa to the south and southeast, and Namibia to the west. The country is a broad tableland, with an average altitude of 3,300 feet. An extensive plateau, extending from near Kenya north to the Zimbabwean border, divides the country into two distinct topographical regions.

Almost the entire remaining portion of the country is covered by the Kalahari Desert. This vast region is characterized by enormous stretches of sand, savanna, and grassland. Although this part of Botswana is only sparsely inhabited by humans, it is one of the richest wildlife regions in all of Africa. Botswana's two largest parks, the Central Kalahari Game Reserve and Gemsbok National Park, are found in this region.

# LESOTHO ("Little Girl and the Monster")

Lesotho is enclosed by South Africa. It has several distinct geographical regions. The western quarter of the country, a plateau averaging 5,000 to 6,000 feet in elevation, ranges from a thin strip only 6 miles wide to a zone 40 miles wide. The soil of this zone is sandstone and is poor and badly eroded.

The remainder of the country is highland. An area of rolling foothills, ranging from 6,000 to 7,000 feet in altitude, forms the border between the lowlands and the mountains in the east. The Maluti Mountains extend north and south. They form a high plateau, 9,000 to 10,000 feet high. The highest point is Thabana Ntlenyana (11,425 feet) in the east. The rich volcanic soils of the foothills and mountains are some of the best in the country.

From *African Legends, Myths, and Folktales for Readers Theatre* by Anthony D. Fredericks. Westport, CT: Teacher Ideas Press. Copyright © 2008.

# SOUTH AFRICA ("How the Tortoise Won Respect"; "Natiki")

South Africa lies at the southernmost part of the African continent. It is bordered on the north by Botswana and Zimbabwe, on the northeast by Mozambique and Swaziland, and on the northwest by Namibia. To the east is the Indian Ocean, and the Atlantic Ocean lies on the western side.

Most of South Africa has elevations of over 3,000 feet. At least 40 percent of the country is at an elevation of over 4,000 feet. The land rises steadily from west to east to the Drakensberg Mountains, the tallest of which is Mont-aux-Sources (10,823 feet). South Africa is another country rich in wildlife and a tourist destination for travelers from all over the world who wish to see elephants, giraffes, antelope, and rhinos in their natural environment.

# NIGERIA ("The Hunter and the Deer-Woman")

Nigeria is situated at the extreme inner corner of the Gulf of Guinea on the west coast of Africa. It borders Chad to the northeast, Cameroon to the east, Benin to the west, Niger to the northwest, and the Atlantic Ocean (Gulf of Guinea) to the south.

Along the entire coastline of Nigeria lies a belt of mangrove swamp forest. Beyond the swamp forest is a wide zone of undulating tropical rain forest. The country then rises to a plateau. Here the vegetation changes from woodland to savanna. In the extreme north, the country begins to touch the southern part of the Sahara Desert.

# LIBERIA ("The Leopard's Daughter")

Located on the west coast of Africa, Liberia is bordered by Guinea on the north, Ivory Coast on the east, Sierra Leone on the northwest, and the Atlantic Ocean on the south and southwest. The country was originally settled by newly freed slaves from the United States immediately after the Civil War.

Liberia has three distinct geographical belts, each of which is parallel to the coast. The low coastal belt is about 50 miles wide, with tidal creeks, shallow lagoons and mangrove marshes. The land then rises abruptly, forming a great belt of high forest with elevations of 600 to 1,000 feet. Inland is a plateau 1,500 to 2,000 feet above sea level, where the forest is dense. The Nimba Mountains, near the Guinea border, rise to 4,200 feet, and the Waulo Mountains to 4,500 feet.

# GHANA ("Anansi's Fishing Expedition")

Ghana is situated on the southern coast of the West African bulge. It is bordered on the east by Togo, on the west by the Ivory Coast, on the south by the Atlantic Ocean, and on the north and northwest by Burkina Fasso.

The coastline consists mostly of low, sandy land, except in the west, where the forest comes down to the sea. The forest belt, which extends northward from the western coast and then eastward into Ashanti for about 170 miles, is broken up into heavily wooded hills and steep ridges. North of the forest is undulating savanna drained by the Black Volta and White Volta Rivers. These rivers join and flow south to the sea through a narrow gap in the hills. Ghana's highest point is at 2,900 feet in a range of hills on the eastern border.

# TOGO ("What Wondrous Powers")

Situated on the west coast of Africa, Togo has land boundaries with Burkina Faso to the north, Benin to the east, and Ghana to the west. On the south it borders the Gulf of Guinea (Atlantic Ocean).

Togo is split in the center by a chain of hills, the Atkora Mountains, extending roughly southwest into Ghana and northeast into Benin. These mountains average about 2,300 feet in height. The highest elevation in the country is Mount Agou (3,235 feet). The 31-mile-long coastline of Togo consists of flat, sandy beaches covered with coconut trees. Much of this area is separated from the mainland by a series of lagoons and lakes.

# Map of Africa

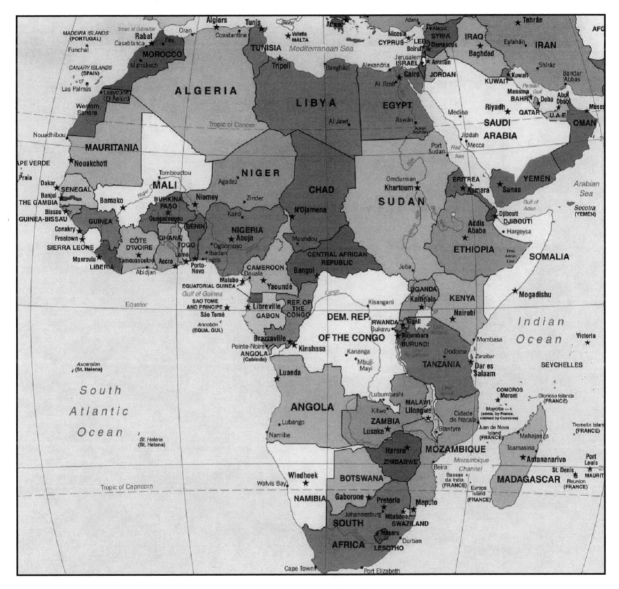

Source: http://www.lib.utexas.edu/maps/africa/africa_pol_2001.pdf

# PART I
# EASTERN AFRICA

Fesito Goes to Market

# Fesito Goes to Market

## (Uganda)

**STAGING:** All of the characters, except Fesito, should be standing. They may have their scripts on music stands or lecterns. The character of Fesito should be seated on a tall stool or chair, or if possible, on a bicycle (feet on the floor) throughout the production. Fesito may move from character to character as the production progresses.

---

| Mama | Musoke | Kasiingi | Kikyo | Bosa | Kagwe |
|------|--------|----------|-------|------|-------|
| X | X | X | X | X | X |
| Fesito→→→ | | | | Waswa | Matabi |
| X | | | | X | X |
| | | | | | Narrator |
| | | | | | X |

**NARRATOR:** The sun rose early one morning and shone into Fesito's eyes. He jumped out of bed with joy in his heart. This was a special day. Because his father was sick in bed with a fever, Fesito had been asked to ride to market on his father's bicycle to deliver bananas. This was a special responsibility, one given only to the men of the village.

**FESITO:** This is a fine day. I will ride the bicycle into town with the bananas. There I will collect the money and bring it back to my family. I will count out all the money, as my father does, and everyone will know that I am an important person. Everyone will know that I am a man of the world!

**MAMA:** Fesito, stop your blabbering. Come and eat your breakfast. You will not go anywhere until you have something in your stomach.

**FESITO:** Yes, mama, I will come and eat my breakfast.

From *African Legends, Myths, and Folktales for Readers Theatre* by Anthony D. Fredericks. Westport, CT: Teacher Ideas Press. Copyright © 2008.

**NARRATOR:** While Fesito was eating his breakfast of porridge, his mother strapped a load of bananas onto the rack of the bicycle. She put some small change into a handkerchief and wrapped it up tight.

**MAMA:** Take this change and take these bananas to market. Be careful and make your family proud.

**FESITO:** Good bye, Mama. I will be back soon.

**NARRATOR:** Fesito pushed the bicycle into the road. He hopped on board and began to ride over the rough and bumpy road. He struggled with the handlebars as the bicycle skidded this way and that way over the slippery ground.

**FESITO:** My father must be very strong to control the bicycle on this slippery road. He must be very strong indeed.

**NARRATOR:** Finally, Fesito came to the top of a hill. He began to plunge down the side of the hill. The bicycle gained speed and was wobbling and spinning and skidding down the slippery slope of the hill.

**FESITO:** Watch out, my friends. Here comes Fesito on his bicycle. Here comes Fesito with his load of bananas for the market. I am riding as a man among men. Wheeeee!

**NARRATOR:** Soon Fesito came to the bottom of the hill and the bicycle began to slow down. Now it was time to pedal. He pushed hard and made good progress along the still slippery road. Soon he came upon old Musoke walking along the side of the road with a load of pawpaws on his back.

**MUSOKE:** Fesito, why is it that you are riding your father's bicycle to market?

**FESITO:** My father is ill, old one. Thus, I am taking the responsibility of getting this load of bananas to market. I am doing a man's job, and I am very proud to do so.

From *African Legends, Myths, and Folktales for Readers Theatre* by Anthony D. Fredericks. Westport, CT: Teacher Ideas Press. Copyright © 2008.

**MUSOKE:** That is good. But as you know, I am an old man and I have a very bad back. I must get my pawpaws to market, but my back hurts me very much. Do you think you could help me?

**FESITO:** I have a heavy load already with the bananas. It would be difficult to ride with more things on my bicycle. But I cannot refuse you, old man. I will take your pawpaws.

**MUSOKE:** Thank you, Fesito. You are very kind to this old man. I shall tell your father what a good man you are.

**NARRATOR:** Fesito tied the pawpaws to the bicycle. The bicycle was even heavier than before. It was difficult riding the bicycle. It was difficult controlling the bicycle. But with great effort Fesito was able to continue down the road.

**KASIINGI:** Fesito! Fesito!

**FESITO:** Who is there? Who is calling my name?

**KASIINGI:** It is I, Kasiingi. I have many things to do today. My day is very busy, and I do not have the time to take my chickens to the market. You are a young boy; can you take my chickens to market?

**FESITO:** I am doing a man's job. I am riding my father's bicycle to market. I am carrying the bananas to market, where they will be sold and where I will collect the money for them. I am not a boy. I am doing a man's job.

**KASIINGI:** I am sorry, Fesito. I did not wish to offend you. But since you are doing a man's job, would you be so kind as to take my three chickens to the market and sell them for me?

**FESITO:** I am carrying many things. My load is very heavy. Where will I carry these chickens?

**KASIINGI:** I will tie these chickens to the very top of your handlebars. They will be very fine there.

**FESITO:** Very well. I do not like this. I do not like this very heavy load that I must now carry to market. But I will do it if it helps out my friends, my neighbors.

**NARRATOR:** And so Fesito continued down the road. His bicycle wobbled all over and was very difficult to control. The load was heavy and he had to travel slower so that he did not tip over. He had to be very careful with the very heavy load. Soon he saw a figure walking ahead of him. It was his friend, Kikyo.

**FESITO:** Hey, Kikyo, where are you going?

**KIKYO:** I am going to the hospital to get some medicine. I need some medicine for my family. It is a long way to the hospital, and I am very tired. Hey, Fesito, let me climb on your bicycle and ride with you into the village.

**FESITO:** Can't you see that I have a very heavy load? I have a load of bananas, a load of pawpaws, and a load of chickens. There is hardly any room on this bicycle for me.

**KIKYO:** I am very small and will not take very much space. I can ride on top of the bananas, and you will not notice me at all. I am very small and very light.

**FESITO:** Okay, my friend. Climb up on top of the bananas and we will go to market together.

**NARRATOR:** And so Fesito, with his heavy load, continued on his way to the market.

**KIKYO:** Hey, Fesito, I am very hungry. May I take just one banana to eat? Just one small banana to eat is all I need.

**FESITO:** Okay, my friend. Just one small banana. But be careful that you do not upset the pile.

**NARRATOR:** And so Kikyo took one small banana and began to eat it. As he was eating, Fesito carefully guided the very heavy bicycle down the road. His heart swelled with pride as he realized that he was carrying a big

From *African Legends, Myths, and Folktales for Readers Theatre* by Anthony D. Fredericks. Westport, CT: Teacher Ideas Press. Copyright © 2008.

load on his father's bicycle, perhaps a bigger load than any other person. He was now a man, he thought. He was strong and was carrying not only bananas to market, but the goods of his neighbors as well.

Just then he saw four boys on the road, four boys he didn't want to see. They were the four boys who were always causing trouble. He knew that there was trouble soon to come.

**BOSA:** Hey, Fesito. What are you doing?

**FESITO:** I am taking my bananas, my pawpaws, and my chickens to market.

**BOSA:** You are loaded with nothing but rubbish. You are nothing but a rubbish collector.

**MATABI:** Yeah, and look who is riding on your bike. It is little Kikyo. He looks like a monkey eating his little banana.

**FESITO:** I think you are jealous of us. We are doing hard work, and you are doing nothing. You are nothing but lazy little boys.

**KAGWE:** I think that we should teach you a lesson. I think you should pay for what you say.

**NARRATOR:** Bosa picked up a long stick. He planned to stick the long stick into the spokes of Fesito's bicycle so that it would send Fesito, Kikyo, and all the things on the bicycle scattering across the ground. Bosa came closer to the bicycle with the stick.

**BOSA:** Ha, you little boy. Now I will make you fall all over the road.

**NARRATOR:** Just then Bosa was hit in the face by a half-eaten banana. He spun to the side of the road, wiping his face.

**KIKYO:** Ha, take that, you little jerk. [to Fesito] Now, my friend, let's ride like the wind.

From *African Legends, Myths, and Folktales for Readers Theatre* by Anthony D. Fredericks. Westport, CT: Teacher Ideas Press. Copyright © 2008.

**MATABI:** You, you are nothing but baboons. Do you think you can be rude to us and get away with it? I will show you who is the boss around here.

**NARRATOR:** Matabi reached for the bunch of bananas. He began to pull the bananas off the bicycle. Just then the chickens pecked him all over his face and all over his arms.

**MATABI:** OUCH! OUCH!! Get away you chickens! Get away!

**FESITO:** Very good. I am so glad that I decided to take the chickens with me on my journey to market.

**NARRATOR:** But they had almost forgotten about Waswa, who picked up a stone and threw it at Fesito.

**WASWA:** Here, take that, you little creep. You are just a bunch of little cowards. Cowards! Cowards! Do you hear me? You are nothing but cowards.

**NARRATOR:** Waswa picked up another stone and was about to throw it at Fesito when, *blonk*, a very large and very ripe pawpaw flew through the air and hit him on his head. Waswa ran into the bushes, yelling and screaming with pain.

**FESITO:** I am glad that I decided to take the pawpaws to market. That was a very good idea. Thank you, Kikyo!

**KIKYO:** Let us ride, Fesito. Let us ride on to market.

**NARRATOR:** Fesito pedaled the bicycle faster and faster. Soon they were at the marketplace. They were laughing and giggling like small children.

**KIKYO:** We did it, my friend. We took care of the bullies and we delivered all our goods to market.

**FESITO:** Yes, we did. Thanks to my thinking and to your good throwing, we made it through the bullies and all the way to the market. We are great friends, but we are even better warriors!

From *African Legends, Myths, and Folktales for Readers Theatre* by Anthony D. Fredericks. Westport, CT: Teacher Ideas Press. Copyright © 2008.

**NARRATOR:** And so Fesito was able to sell all the bananas, all the pawpaws, and all the chickens in the market. He took all the money and climbed back on his bicycle and began to ride home. He laughed and laughed all the way home. He was now a man among men. His father would be very proud of him.

From *African Legends, Myths, and Folktales for Readers Theatre* by Anthony D. Fredericks. Westport, CT: Teacher Ideas Press. Copyright © 2008.

The Lion, the Hare, and the Hyena

# The Lion, the Hare, and the Hyena

## (Kenya)

**STAGING:** Each of the characters should be seated on a tall stool or chair. Each narrator should be posted behind a lectern or podium. For effect, you may wish to have some dried chicken bones as props for this story.

---

```
                    Lion
                     X
        Hare                      Hyena
         X                          X
              (bones)                          Narrator 1      Narrator 2
                                                   X               X
```

**NARRATOR 1:** Once, in a faraway place, there lived a mighty lion. Now this lion was very strong and had little trouble catching enough food to eat. But one day while he was hunting for antelope, he stepped into a meerkat's hole and injured his leg. He limped back to his cave, but soon realized that getting food would be very difficult. He began to worry.

**NARRATOR 2:** Now, as luck would have it, he had a friend, the hare. And, as luck would have it, his friend happened to pass by the lion's cave one day.

**HARE:** Hey, my friend, what is the matter?

**LION:** I have hurt myself while hunting. I do not know how I will be able to survive.

**HARE:** Well, that's what friends are for. I will care for you until you are well enough to hunt on your own.

From *African Legends, Myths, and Folktales for Readers Theatre* by Anthony D. Fredericks. Westport, CT: Teacher Ideas Press. Copyright © 2008.

**NARRATOR 1:** And so the hare cared for his friend, the lion. Under his care, the lion gradually returned to good health. Slowly his strength came back, enough so that he could capture small animals for both of them to eat. It was not long before there was a pile of bones outside the cave.

**NARRATOR 2:** But as you well know, that would not be the end of our story. For there is another character you must know. An extremely unsavory character: the hyena. Now the hyena was looking for his supper when his nose picked up the scent of the bones scattered in front of the lion's cave. He crept up to the cave and saw the delicious bones, but being a very cowardly creature he decided that he should use some form of trickery to get the bones he desired. He decided that it might be best to try and make friends with the lion.

**HYENA:** Greetings, your great majesty. You are indeed the strongest and wisest creature in all the land, and I am honored to have stumbled upon your cave. I trust that you are well and that your belly is always full.

**LION:** [angrily] Who goes there? Oh, I see it is you, hyena. I should capture you now and eat you for my evening meal. But there is not enough meat on your skinny bones, and it would be such a bother to capture you.

**HYENA:** Oh, great lion, I am your friend. I bring you no harm. I bring you no harsh words. I have only come to tell you how much you have been missed by the other animals. We are all looking for your return to good health and your happiness.

**LION:** [angrily] Get out! Get out! If you had really been interested in my health, you would have come to see me a long time ago when I was first injured. You are a sly, cunning creature. You are a bother. Get out! Get out, I say!

From *African Legends, Myths, and Folktales for Readers Theatre* by Anthony D. Fredericks. Westport, CT: Teacher Ideas Press. Copyright © 2008.

**NARRATOR 1:** And so the hyena slunk off into the evening with his tail tucked up under his legs. He could not sway the lion. And he could not get close enough to the pile of bones to steal them away.

**HYENA:** I shall try again. I shall try again. There must be some way I can get those bones.

**NARRATOR 2:** A few days later the hyena saw his chance. The Hare had gone off to fetch some water to use in cooking the evening meal. The hyena once again approached the lion.

**LION:** Who goes there? What do you want?

**HYENA:** It is only I, my friend.

**LION:** [angrily] Friend! Friend!! How can you call me friend? You are nothing but a cur. You are not a friend.

**HYENA:** But, you see, I am. For I am told that your wounded leg is not healing as well as it should. I have heard that it is taking a long time to mend. It is, I have heard, perhaps the result of some poor treatment you are receiving from your friend, your so-called friend, the hare.

**LION:** What are you talking about? If it were not for my friend, the hare, I would not be doing well at all. I may have starved to death. I may have died. My friend helped me. He helped me while you were out in the wild. He helped me, and where were you? If you were my friend, why were you not here to care for me?

**HYENA:** What I have said is the truth. It is known among all the creatures that the hare is not providing for your best interests. It is known that he is not giving you the best care. It is known that he is giving you the wrong treatment for your injury. You must be warned, my friend. Your friend the hare does not have your best interests at heart.

 From *African Legends, Myths, and Folktales for Readers Theatre* by Anthony D. Fredericks. Westport, CT: Teacher Ideas Press. Copyright © 2008.

**NARRATOR 1:** At that moment the hare returned from the river with his gourd filled with water.

**HARE:** Well, hyena, what a surprise to see you here again. What could you want from us?

**LION:** The hyena has told a remarkable story. He has told me that your skills as a doctor are known far and wide throughout the countryside. He has told me that the medicines you use are the finest in the whole countryside. But he also tells me that my wounded leg could have been cured a very long time ago. You could have healed it with powerful medicines much sooner than you are now doing.

**NARRATOR 2:** The hare thought very carefully. He knew of the hyena's cunning, and he was sure that the hyena was trying to trick them. He spoke with care.

**HARE:** Well, that may be true, and that may not be true.

**LION:** What are you saying?

**HARE:** Well, it is true that I am a very small animal and many of the medicines that I use are very large. Sometimes there is great difficulty in obtaining the proper medicines. For example, the proper medicines for my friend, the lion.

**LION:** What do you mean?

**HARE:** [to the lion] Well, in order for your injury to heal its best, I need a section of skin from the back of an adult hyena to place on your injury. That is the only way it will properly heal.

**NARRATOR 1:** Hearing those words, the Lion leaped onto the hyena. He quickly tore a section of skin off the hyena's back, from the top of his head to the tip of his tail. He wrapped the skin around his injured leg.

**NARRATOR 2:** The wounded leg healed very quickly, and the lion was able to hunt and survive, thanks to his friend, the hare.

From *African Legends, Myths, and Folktales for Readers Theatre* by Anthony D. Fredericks. Westport, CT: Teacher Ideas Press. Copyright © 2008.

**NARRATOR 1:** The hyena, however, could not show his face. He had been humiliated, and he hid out among the trees and bushes, as he continues to hide today.

**NARRATOR 2:** And if you look very carefully, you will see that the hairs on the back of the hyena—where his skin was torn away by the lion—are stretched and stand on end. To this day, every hyena has long, coarse hairs on its back. They are there to remind us that the hyena is never to be trusted. He continues to be a crafty fellow, but he is never to be trusted!

From *African Legends, Myths, and Folktales for Readers Theatre* by Anthony D. Fredericks. Westport, CT: Teacher Ideas Press. Copyright © 2008.

Tiyotiyo

# Tiyotiyo

## (Zimbabwe)

**STAGING:** The two narrators may be standing at lecterns or podiums. The four human characters may all be seated on tall stools or chairs. The two birds may be standing off to the side of the staging area.

```
Narrator 1                                                    Narrator 2
   X                                                              X
Old Muto          Gano          Kondo          Old Marumba
   X                X              X                X
                                                 Bird 1      Bird 2
                                                   X            X
```

**NARRATOR 1:** It was long, long ago when there was a village of people who lived their lives entirely on meat, fruits, wild animals, and roots.

**NARRATOR 2:** These people did not know about grain, nor did they even know about how to plant grain.

**NARRATOR 1:** Now in this village there lived a young man by the name of Gano. Gano was a helpful boy, but he had an injured leg that prevented him from traveling very far from home.

**NARRATOR 2:** Gano lived with his grandfather, Old Muto. Old Muto was very, very old and could do very little except sit in the sun every day and watch the people work.

**NARRATOR 1:** Because Gano could not hunt, and because Old Muto was far too old, the two of them would often go hungry.

**NARRATOR 2:** There were some days when Gano would go into the bush to search for wild fruits or locusts. He would

From *African Legends, Myths, and Folktales for Readers Theatre* by Anthony D. Fredericks. Westport, CT: Teacher Ideas Press. Copyright © 2008.

also look for bird's eggs to take back to his grandfather.

**NARRATOR 1:** But Gano did not like stealing bird's eggs from the nests he found. He often felt as though these eggs were as unprotected as he was, and he took great pity on them.

**NARRATOR 2:** But one day Gano was out in the bush and he heard the sweet sound of a bird in danger. The bird burst into the open and then fell to the ground. It beat its wings against the ground and made many loud sounds. It flew up and then fell to the ground. It flew up once again and then fell to the ground once again.

**NARRATOR 1:** Gano rushed over to the bird and gently picked it up. He noticed that one of its legs was broken. He carefully tucked the bird into the folds of his robe.

**NARRATOR 2:** It was then that he heard the sound of barking dogs. It was a hunting party looking for game. Gano struggled up into the branches of a nearby muonde tree and waited for the hunting party to pass by.

**NARRATOR 1:** The hunting party was led by Kondo, the one person in the village that Gano hated most. Kondo was always unkind and always had many harsh things to say to Gano.

**KONDO:** [angrily, to Gano] Get down from that tree. Get down from that tree and give me the bird you have tucked into your robe.

**GANO:** What bird? What bird are you talking about?

**KONDO:** Give me the bird you have hidden in the folds of your robe! Give me the bird, or I will shoot you down with an arrow.

**GANO:** Go ahead. Just go ahead and shoot me with your arrow.

From *African Legends, Myths, and Folktales for Readers Theatre* by Anthony D. Fredericks. Westport, CT: Teacher Ideas Press. Copyright © 2008.

**NARRATOR 2:** It was just then that Old Marumba was passing by. Old Marumba was searching for medicinal herbs to take back to the village.

**OLD MARUMBA:** Let him keep the bird, Kondo. There are always plenty of birds. You will be able to find another bird somewhere on your hunt.

**NARRATOR 1:** Kondo respected his elders, even if he didn't like what they said. Old Marumba was old, and although Kondo didn't want to leave Gano alone, he obeyed the old man and went on his way down the path.

**GANO:** Thank you, old man. You have saved my life from that mean Kondo.

**OLD MARUMBA:** You are welcome, young man. You are very welcome.

**GANO:** I am thinking about leaving the village. Life here is difficult. I cannot hunt like the others, and it is hard finding enough food for my grandfather and myself.

**OLD MARUMBA:** You should not act hastily, young Gano. You are a bright young man. You are an important member of our village. You should stay.

**NARRATOR 2:** Gano limped on home. There, he worked to help the bird. He treated the bird's broken leg by cleaning it and by putting a splint of two bamboo pieces on it.

**NARRATOR 1:** The days passed by, and each day Gano treated the bird. As he worked with the bird, he talked to it. He told the bird stories. He told the birds about the old days in the village. He told the bird some of his dreams and some of his wishes. He would speak to the bird every day.

**GANO:** You are a pretty bird. Where do you live? How do you survive? Who is your mate?

**NARRATOR 2:** Every day young Gano would talk to the bird. Then one day, the bird said something to Gano.

**BIRD 1:** Tiyotiyo. (Ti-Yo-Ti-Yo).

From *African Legends, Myths, and Folktales for Readers Theatre* by Anthony D. Fredericks. Westport, CT: Teacher Ideas Press. Copyright © 2008.

**GANO:** [surprised] You have talked to me! You have talked to me!

**BIRD 1:** Tiyotiyo.

**GANO:** You have said, "Wait a little longer."

**BIRD 1:** Tiyotiyo. Tiyotiyo.

**GANO:** Wait a little longer. I will do so. I will do so, just as you say.

**NARRATOR 1:** Now at that time several men of the village went out on a hunting trip. They were led by Kondo. They were away for a very long time: three weeks. Nobody had heard any news of them. They had been away for much longer than any other hunting party.

**NARRATOR 2:** The women of the village were sad. They wished for their husbands to come home. Their husbands had been in the bush for a very long time. The women were sad. The women were anxious.

**NARRATOR 1:** Gano heard of the plight of the women. He wanted to help them, but he didn't know what he could do.

**NARRATOR 2:** Then one day, after the little bird had completely healed, it flew off into the nearby hills. Gano followed the bird. When he came over the hills he saw a field of strange grass, a strange grass that bore little brown grains.

**GANO:** What is this?

**BIRD 1:** Tiyotiyo.

**NARRATOR 1:** It was then that Gano knew that he should gather up the grains. He did this and placed all the grains on top of a large, flat rock.

**BIRD 1:** Tiyotiyo.

**NARRATOR 2:** Gano listened carefully and knew just what to do. He took another rock and began to grind the grain. He began to grind the grain into flour.

From *African Legends, Myths, and Folktales for Readers Theatre* by Anthony D. Fredericks. Westport, CT: Teacher Ideas Press. Copyright © 2008.

**NARRATOR 1:** As Gano was grinding the grain into flour, the little bird flew to a nearby river. It gathered up water in its beak and brought it over to the rock. It flew between the river and the rock many times. Each time it brought more water.

**BIRD 1:** Tiyotiyo.

**GANO:** I hear you. Now, you are telling me that I should mix the flour and the water together.

**NARRATOR 2:** Gano mixed the flour and water together into a thick paste. Afterward, the bird showed Gano a hacha fruit tree.

**BIRD 1:** Tiyotiyo.

**GANO:** I understand. I am to collect the hacha and mix it with the paste.

**NARRATOR 1:** Gano peeled the hacha and squeezed the juice.

**BIRD 1:** Tiyotiyo.

**NARRATOR 2:** Gano added the juice to the paste and patted the mixture into small cakes. He placed the small cakes in the sun to dry.

**BIRD 1:** Tiyotiyo.

**NARRATOR 1:** Soon the cakes were dried. Gano tasted one of them and thought that it was the most wonderful food he had ever eaten.

**GANO:** Now, I will no longer be hungry. I will never have to worry about being unable to hunt.

**BIRD 1:** Tiyotiyo.

**NARRATOR 2:** Gano knew from the sound of his friend, the bird, that he must take a long journey.

**NARRATOR 1:** So they traveled a long way. They traveled over many roads. They traveled over many hills and many mountains. They traveled until they reached the mouth of a large cave. The mouth of the cave had been filled with many rocks and rubble.

**BIRD 1:** Tiyotiyo.

**GANO:** Ah, my friend, you are telling me that I must push aside the rocks from the mouth of this cave.

**NARRATOR 2:** And so Gano, using all his strength, began to push away all the rocks from the mouth of the cave.

**NARRATOR 1:** Inside the cave were Kondo and all his dogs and all his fellow hunters.

**KONDO:** You have saved us, brave Gano. We came to this cave because we were following a strange bird. When we came inside, the entrance fell in behind us and we were trapped. We did not know if we would ever escape. But you saved us.

**BIRD 1:** Tiyotiyo.

**GANO:** I understand. [to the men] Now please eat some of these cakes that I have prepared. You must be very hungry.

**KONDO:** Thank you. Thank you very much.

**BIRD 2:** Tiyotiyo.

**GANO:** I understand. You lured the hunters into the cave and made the entrance fall in.

**BIRD 2:** Tiyotiyo.

**GANO:** You wanted to teach them a lesson.

**BIRD 1 & BIRD 2:** Tiyotiyo. Tiyotiyo.

**GANO:** [to the men] Come, my friends. There is something I wish to show you.

**NARRATOR 2:** The two birds flew ahead. Gano followed them. And the hunters followed Gano.

**NARRATOR 1:** The birds led them to a vast plain where the strange grass grew. It was the same grass that Gano used to make the sweet cakes.

**GANO:** Kondo, take your hunters and return home. Tell everyone about this field of grass. Tell them to come here.

**KONDO:** Yes, my new friend. I will tell them as you wish.

**NARRATOR 2:** And so Kondo returned home and brought all the people to the field of grass.

**NARRATOR 1:** And from that day forth the people of the village learned how to grow grain. And they never went hungry again.

**NARRATOR 2:** And they celebrated the two birds in song and in legend. And even today, the people of the village sing of the two birds—two pigeons—who led them to a new life.

**BIRD 1 & BIRD 2:** Tiyotiyo. Tiyotiyo.

From *African Legends, Myths, and Folktales for Readers Theatre* by Anthony D. Fredericks. Westport, CT: Teacher Ideas Press. Copyright © 2008.

The Hare's Revenge

# The Hare's Revenge

## (Zambia)

**STAGING:** The characters should all be seated on chairs or tall stools. They may hold their scripts in their hands, or the scripts may be placed on music stands. The Buffalo should talk in a brusque voice, while the Hare should speak in a quiet voice.

---

```
                    Buffalo           Hare
                       X               X
                                                          Lion
                                                           X
          Narrator
             X
```

**NARRATOR:** It was a fine spring day. The buffalo was on his way to see the chief of all animals, the lion. As he was walking down the road, he chanced upon the hare, who was skipping and hopping across the countryside.

**BUFFALO:** Hey, hare. Would you like to come with me to visit my old friend the lion?

**HARE:** I hear the lion is a very fierce chief. He eats subjects whom he does not like. I am afraid for my life. The lion chief will surely eat me if I go with you on your journey. It is far too dangerous. I cannot go.

**BUFFALO:** You have nothing to be afraid of. The lion may be chief, but he is also an old friend of mine. He will listen to what I say. There will be no danger to you at all.

**HARE:** I do not understand. Why would you want me to travel with you to see the lion?

**BUFFALO:** I should like for you to carry my sleeping mat. As you know, I am a very important animal, and it is not right for important animals such as I to carry our own sleeping mats. If you would carry my sleeping mat, I should be very grateful. And besides, I would reward you quite well.

**HARE:** Very well. I shall carry your sleeping mat. And I shall journey with you to see the lion.

**NARRATOR:** So it was. The buffalo placed his sleeping mat on the shoulders of the hare. Then, they both continued down the road to the lion's place. The sun was very hot overhead, and the hare got very tired.

**HARE:** Your sleeping mat is very heavy, my friend. I do not think that I can carry it the whole way to the lion's hut. Perhaps you can help me with this heavy load.

**BUFFALO:** [angrily] You complain too much, hare. Stop all your complaining. It is just a sleeping mat. It should not be too heavy for someone like you.

**HARE:** I do not think that I can walk much farther. The sun is hot, we have walked far, and your mat is heavy.

**BUFFALO:** [very angrily and in a loud voice] STOP! Stop all your complaining. Let us continue on.

**NARRATOR:** The buffalo and the hare continued down the road. The hare was much too afraid to say anything to the buffalo. He walked along in silence.

Finally, it was the middle of the day. The buffalo and the hare stopped under a large tree to eat their midday meal and to rest in the shade. As the hare put his load beneath the tree, he was very thankful for this opportunity to rest. However, as he lay down his head he heard a buzzing sound. He looked around and saw some bees buzzing nearby. He arose and walked over to a hive hidden inside a hole in the ground.

From *African Legends, Myths, and Folktales for Readers Theatre* by Anthony D. Fredericks. Westport, CT: Teacher Ideas Press. Copyright © 2008.

**HARE:** I have found a great treasure. I am so hungry that I must eat all that I can.

**NARRATOR:** And so the hare filled his mouth with sweet honey. He tiptoed back to the tree, but just then the buffalo awoke from his nap.

**BUFFALO:** We must be on our way. We cannot delay. Here, take my sleeping mat upon your shoulders and we shall be on our way. We must arrive at the village before the sun sets in the west.

**NARRATOR:** The two traveling companions set off down the road. But just then the hare had a clever thought. He stopped and scampered back to the bee's hive.

**BUFFALO:** [angrily] Where are you going? We must be on our way.

**HARE:** Do not worry, my friend. I have decided to fill my pot with some extra honey that I found. It will serve us well on our journey, and we can present some to the lion as a gift.

**BUFFALO:** Very well. As you wish.

**NARRATOR:** The hare had grown very tired of the buffalo and his mean temper. He had thought of a way to get even with the demanding buffalo. When he got back to the hive, he filled his pot to the brim with more honey. Then he unrolled the sleeping mat and spread a great many bees over the surface. He carefully rolled up the mat and hurried after the buffalo.

**BUFFALO:** Greetings again. What were you doing?

**HARE:** Oh, nothing. I just wanted to prepare a special surprise.

**NARRATOR:** Before long the buffalo and the hare arrived at the village of the lion.

 From *African Legends, Myths, and Folktales for Readers Theatre* by Anthony D. Fredericks. Westport, CT: Teacher Ideas Press. Copyright © 2008.

**LION:** Welcome, friends. Welcome to my village. You both must be very tired after your long journey. Let us eat and then you shall rest.

**NARRATOR:** The lion presented the two companions with a wonderful feast. There was music and dancing and singing and laughter long into the night.

**LION:** Now it is time to rest. You are tired, and we have many things to talk about tomorrow. Here is a hut. Please enter and enjoy a peaceful rest.

**HARE:** The night is very warm. I should prefer to sleep outside on the grass.

**LION:** As you wish.

**BUFFALO:** I shall sleep inside the hut. Please close the door tightly as you depart so that I will not be disturbed by any noise or visitors.

**NARRATOR:** The hare closed the door of the hut and made sure that it was fastened quite securely. He giggled and he laughed as he hopped off into the bushes to await the fate of his traveling companion. It wasn't long before bellows and shouts came forth from the hut. For the buffalo had unrolled his sleeping mat only to discover that it was filled with angry, stinging bees.

**BUFFALO:** HELP! HELP!! HELP!!!

LET ME OUT! LET ME OUT!! LET ME OUT!!!

**NARRATOR:** The lion heard the shouts and quickly raced back to the hut. Using all his strength, he pushed open the door. His friend, the buffalo, came dashing out of the hut with a swarm of bees close behind. He ran into the woods, across a long field, and over several hills before the swarm left him. Then, hanging his head, he limped back to the lion's village.

**LION:** What happened, my friend?

From *African Legends, Myths, and Folktales for Readers Theatre* by Anthony D. Fredericks. Westport, CT: Teacher Ideas Press. Copyright © 2008.

**BUFFALO:** [angrily] It was the hare. He was the one who rolled up the bees in my sleeping mat. If I ever catch him, he will truly be sorry for what he did. I can't wait to catch him!

**NARRATOR:** By that time the hare was far, far away. From then on, he was very careful to keep his distance from the buffalo, which is why today you never see them traveling together.

The Enchanting Song of the Magical Bird

# The Enchanting Song of the Magical Bird

## (Tanzania)

**STAGING:** The three narrators should all be seated on tall stools. Each should be posted behind a music stand or lectern. The chief should be standing and may walk about the staging area during the presentation.

---

|  | Narrator 1 | Narrator 2 | Narrator 3 |
|---|---|---|---|
|  | X | X | X |
| Chief |  |  |  |
| X |  |  |  |

**NARRATOR 1:** It was in the old times, when there was a village that was tucked into the lush green hills of our country. The villagers were very happy, and the land was fertile with good crops. Everyone lived very well, and there was joy among the people.

**NARRATOR 2:** But one day, from somewhere in the east there arrived a very strange but very beautiful bird. It was a large bird, and it took from the villagers.

**NARRATOR 3:** It swooped down and took their chickens and their goats. It swooped down and it ate their crops and their fruit. It swooped down and broke into their granaries and their storehouses and stole all their food supplies for the winter.

**NARRATOR 1:** There was much crying in the village.

**NARRATOR 2:** The people were very sad.

**NARRATOR 3:** Misery swept through the village and over the lush hills.

From *African Legends, Myths, and Folktales for Readers Theatre* by Anthony D. Fredericks. Westport, CT: Teacher Ideas Press. Copyright © 2008.

**NARRATOR 1:** No one could catch the bird. He was too elusive and too fast.

**NARRATOR 2:** Even the strongest men in the village could not get their hands on the bird.

**NARRATOR 3:** The bird was far too quick for anyone to catch.

**NARRATOR 1:** The villagers rarely saw the bird, but they could hear the flapping of its wings as it came to rest in the high branches of the yellowwood tree. It hid in the thick canopy of leaves high in the tree.

**NARRATOR 2:** Now the chief of the village was very angry. He was very frustrated. The bird was helping itself to everything the villagers had worked for.

**NARRATOR 3:** The bird had even targeted the storehouse of the chief. It had taken all his winter supplies and all his livestock. The chief was very angry and very mad at the strange bird.

**CHIEF:** Oh, terrible bird, you bring great misery to our village. You make us all very angry. We shall cut you down. We shall bring you to earth. I now order all the men of the village to get their axes and their machetes. You will all move against the bird. You will cut down the yellowwood tree. Cut down the tree! Cut down the tree! That is the answer. Cut down the tree!

**NARRATOR 1:** With sharp axes and sharp machetes in their hands, the men of the village approached the yellowwood tree. Their axes dug into the bark of the tree. Their machetes bit into the flesh of the tree. The tree shook with the power of their blows.

**NARRATOR 2:** The tree shuttered with the force of their mighty blows.

**NARRATOR 3:** The tree bent to the force of their powerful blows.

From *African Legends, Myths, and Folktales for Readers Theatre* by Anthony D. Fredericks. Westport, CT: Teacher Ideas Press. Copyright © 2008.

**NARRATOR 1:** But from the tree came a honey-sweet song. The music reached out to the men. The music reached far into their hearts. The music sang to them of precious things that would never return.

**NARRATOR 2:** The song was so sweet and so precious that the men dropped their machetes. The men dropped their axes. One by one they fell to the ground.

**NARRATOR 3:** All the men fell to their knees and stared up into the branches of the tree. They stared in longing and yearning for the bird, who sang to them in all its splendor and majesty.

**NARRATOR 1:** The hearts of the men became soft, and the hands of the men became weak.

**NARRATOR 2:** How could a bird so beautiful and so lovely cause so much damage and destruction?

**NARRATOR 3:** Like sleepwalkers, the men shuffled back to the village. They approached the chief and told him that they could not harm such a beautiful and lovely creature.

**CHIEF:** Why do you say this? The bird is bringing great harm to our village. He takes our crops. He takes our livestock. He steals from us every day. We must break his power. I will get the young men of the village to assist me. The young men will break the power of the bird.

**NARRATOR 1:** And so the next morning the young men of the village took their axes and took their machetes and set off for the tree.

**NARRATOR 2:** Their blows slammed into the tree. The axes bit into the bark. The machetes dug deep into the flesh of the tree. The tree shuddered with the blows.

**NARRATOR 3:** But just as before, the leaves of the yellowwood tree parted and the strange bird appeared in all its wonder and splendor. Once again, a most beautiful song came from the bird, a sweet melody that echoed over the hills and down through the valleys.

**NARRATOR 1:** The young men listed to the enchanting song. It was a song that spoke to them of love, and strength, and heroic deeds yet to be done.

**NARRATOR 2:** This bird could not be bad, they thought. It is not a wicked bird. It is not a terrible creature.

**NARRATOR 3:** And so the arms of the young men became weak. The machetes and axes fell from their hands onto the ground. They knelt before the bird and listened quietly to its beautiful song. That night, bewildered and amazed, they stumbled back to the village, the mysterious song of the bird still soft in their ears.

**CHIEF:** Why can't you fell the tree? Why can you not chop down the tree and rid us of this powerful bird? You are all strong, but you cannot rid our village of this bird! Now there are only the children of our village left. Their hearing is pure. Their eyes are clear. I will take them myself to the tree, and we will get rid of this evil bird.

**NARRATOR 1:** The sun rose brightly the next morning. The village chief gathered together all the children of the village and went to the yellowwood tree where the bird was resting. The first child swung his axe into the bark of the tree.

**NARRATOR 2:** At just that moment, the leaves of the tree parted and the mysterious bird appeared. It was the most beautiful creature in all the land.

**NARRATOR 3:** But the children did not look up at the bird. They continued to swing their axes. They continued to swing their machetes. They chopped, and chopped, and chopped.

**CHIEF:** I hear such a beautiful sound from the tree. I hear such a beautiful sound from the bird. The bird's song is so sweet. The bird's song is so lovely. It is the sweetest sound in the land.

From *African Legends, Myths, and Folktales for Readers Theatre* by Anthony D. Fredericks. Westport, CT: Teacher Ideas Press. Copyright © 2008.

**NARRATOR 1:** But the children's ears could not hear the sound of the bird.

**NARRATOR 2:** The children's ears could only hear the chop, chop, chop of their axes.

**NARRATOR 3:** The children's ears could only hear the whack, whack, whack of their machetes.

**NARRATOR 1:** In a short time the trunk of the yellowwood tree began to crack and creak. With a great moan it crashed to the ground. Thunder rang out everywhere. When the chief looked among the branches, he found the mysterious bird, dead. It had been crushed to death by the enormous weight of the yellowwood tree.

**NARRATOR 2:** The people of the village came running to the tree. No one could believe what they saw. No one could believe what the children had accomplished.

**NARRATOR 3:** And that night there was a great feast. There was a great feast to celebrate and reward the children of the village. The songs of the villagers rang out over the hills. The songs of the villagers swept down through the valleys.

**CHIEF:** The children are strong. The children have eyes that are clear. The children have ears that can truly hear. Let us celebrate the children of our village. They are the eyes and ears of our people! Let us celebrate!

From *African Legends, Myths, and Folktales for Readers Theatre* by Anthony D. Fredericks. Westport, CT: Teacher Ideas Press. Copyright © 2008.

The Cat Who Came Indoors

# The Cat Who Came Indoors

## (Zimbabwe)

**STAGING:** All the characters should be standing with scripts in their hands or placed on music stands. The narrator may be seated on a tall stool or chair.

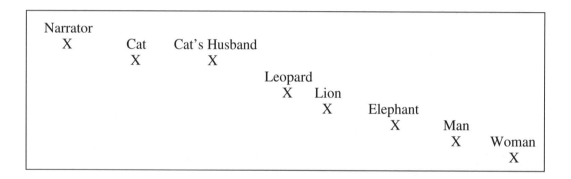

**NARRATOR:** This is a long-ago story. It is a story that answers a question, a persistent question that all have asked, but few have answered. So, now let us begin. For you see, in this long ago time there lived a cat, a very wild cat who lived alone deep in the bush. Getting tired of living alone, she took herself a husband. Now, she thought that her husband was the finest creature in all the land.

**CAT:** Yes, my husband is the finest creature in all the land.

**CAT'S HUSBAND:** I am happy to be the husband of such a fine cat. She is a good wife.

**NARRATOR:** So one day the cat and her husband were strolling along. The sun was bright overhead and they were both happy. Suddenly a great leopard jumped out of the grass and onto the back of the husband.

 From *African Legends, Myths, and Folktales for Readers Theatre* by Anthony D. Fredericks. Westport, CT: Teacher Ideas Press. Copyright © 2008.

**CAT'S HUSBAND:** Owwww! That hurt!

**LEOPARD:** I just wanted to let you know who was the strongest animal in the whole jungle. It is I, the leopard.

**NARRATOR:** The cat looked at her husband, all covered with dirt and grass.

**CAT:** Ohhh. It looks like my husband is not the strongest animal in the jungle. He is not as strong as I first believed. He is dirty and muddy and not very handsome at all.

**NARRATOR:** And so the cat went to live with the leopard.

**CAT:** We are living a very happy life. I now have a strong husband, someone who will protect me from all possible enemies.

**NARRATOR:** So the cat and her new husband went out to look for some food one day. Suddenly—whoosh—a large and very angry lion jumped out of the grass and onto the leopard's back.

**LION:** I am the strongest animal in the jungle. Anyone who says different shall feel the wrath of my claws and the power of my teeth.

**CAT:** You are, indeed, a very strong animal. I did not know how strong you really were.

**LION:** I am stronger than strong. I am the strongest there is.

**CAT:** Hmmmm. I guess the leopard is not as strong as I thought he was. Lion is far stronger.

**NARRATOR:** And so, as you might guess, the cat went to live with the lion. Well, things went very well for the lion and the cat. But then one day they decided to go for a walk in the dark forest. As they walked along, they suddenly heard a very big sound. Crush! Crash! Crunch! It was the elephant. And before they knew what was happening the elephant, put one foot on top of the lion and squashed him flat.

**CAT:** Ohhh. It seems as though the lion is not as strong as I thought he was. It seems as though the elephant is much stronger.

**ELEPHANT:** Yes, I am the strongest animal in the whole jungle. I am stronger than any other animal there is.

**NARRATOR:** And so it was that the cat went to live with the elephant. Each day she would gently climb up between the elephant's ears and go to sleep. She would purr between his ears and was very happy.

**CAT:** I like sleeping between the ears of my new husband. It is warm and comfortable.

**NARRATOR:** And so it was that the cat and the elephant were very happy. That is, until one day when they went down to the river to get a cool drink of water. As they were moving through the tall reeds, they heard a loud bang. It was a shot from a gun, and with that shot the elephant fell to the ground, dead.

**CAT:** Ohhh. I see that the elephant is not the strongest in the jungle. Somebody else is stronger than the elephant. Who could it be?

**MAN:** It is I. I am stronger than any animal because I have a gun. The gun makes me very strong and someone to be feared by every animal in the jungle.

**CAT:** Ohhh. I can see that you are stronger than any of my husbands. You are, indeed, the strongest animal in the whole of the jungle.

**NARRATOR:** And so it was that the cat walked along beside the man as he made his way home. When they reached the hut of the man, the cat leaped up onto the roof and curled up in the sun.

**CAT:** I must have found the finest of all creatures in the jungle. This shall be a fine place for me.

From *African Legends, Myths, and Folktales for Readers Theatre* by Anthony D. Fredericks. Westport, CT: Teacher Ideas Press. Copyright © 2008.

**NARRATOR:** The cat lived very contentedly on the roof of the man's hut. She could catch mice that scampered over the thatch and she could catch rats that fell down from the trees overhead. But then one day as she rested on the roof she heard a great noise coming from the hut.

**WOMAN:** Get out! Get out! You are no good. You do not work. You are so lazy that I am tired of you.

**NARRATOR:** The cat peered over the edge of the roof. She saw that the man and a woman were arguing and yelling and screaming. Their voices grew louder and louder. Finally, out came the man, tumbling head over heels in the dust.

**WOMAN:** Get out of my house!. You are no good! Do you hear me? You are no good!

**CAT:** Hmmm. Now I think I know who is the most powerful creature in all of the jungle. I think it is Woman.

**NARRATOR:** And on that day the cat came down from her perch on the roof. She crept inside the hut and curled up next to the fire. And that is where she has been ever since.

From *African Legends, Myths, and Folktales for Readers Theatre* by Anthony D. Fredericks. Westport, CT: Teacher Ideas Press. Copyright © 2008.

# PART II
# MIDDLE AFRICA

The Boy Who Wanted the Moon

# The Boy Who Wanted the Moon

## (Congo)

**STAGING:** The narrator may stand at a lectern or podium in the front of the staging area. The other characters may be walking around (with their scripts in their hands). They should talk to each other rather than to the audience.

---

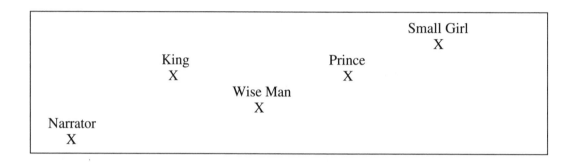

**NARRATOR:** Many years ago, long before I was born, there lived in our land a great king. This king was very rich and he had many children. But he only had one son, a prince, and to him he gave everything. He gave him his own house, his own servants, and many riches that only a king can give. He gave him almost everything he owned because he loved his son very much. But the son wanted more. He wanted more and more. And he became very selfish. The son made all the other children watch him while he took a nap each day. He made all the other children watch him as he ate his meals every day. And he made all the other children watch him as he washed his face and put on his finest robes each day.

**PRINCE:** [haughtily] I am the greatest human who has ever lived. My father gives me much because I am so beautiful and wise and deserving. I am a prince, but one day I shall be king because I have so much. I have many things now, but I will have even more when I am king. I have everything I want. I have everything, indeed.

**SMALL GIRL:** No, you do not. You do not have everything!

**PRINCE:** Who says this? Who says I do not have everything?

**SMALL GIRL:** I do. I say you do not have everything.

**PRINCE:** You are wrong and you shall be punished. I am the prince, who will be king, and I have everything. If you think you're so smart, tell me one thing, just one thing that I do not have.

**SMALL GIRL:** You do not have the moon.

**NARRATOR:** With that, all the people in the village, even the children, began to laugh at the prince. He became very angry and stomped off to see his father.

**PRINCE:** Oh father, the people make fun of me because I do not have the moon. I want the moon. I want the moon right now!

**KING:** That is impossible. You cannot have the moon. No one can ever have the moon.

**PRINCE:** I want the moon. I WANT THE MOON!

**KING:** You are not serious. No one, not even you, can have the moon.

**PRINCE:** I WANT THE MOON!

**KING:** I cannot give you the moon. I can give you everything you want, but I cannot give you the moon. It is impossible.

**NARRATOR:** It was then that the prince began to cry. He cried and cried and cried. For a long time, he sobbed and sobbed. The king became very worried. He had never seen his son this way. He had tried to always give his son everything he wanted, but now his son was very sad.

**PRINCE:** [sadly] If you do not give me the moon I will be sad for the rest of my life. I will hide in my hut and never come out. I will cry and I will be sad.

**NARRATOR:** The king became very worried. He did not want his son, the prince, to be sad. He wanted his son to have everything. So he decided to go to the wise man of the village and ask his advice.

**KING:** Oh, wise man, my son is very sad. He wants to have the moon. How can I give him the moon?

**WISE MAN:** You are not serious. You must be making a joke.

**KING:** I am not making a joke. I want to give my son the moon. He is very sad without it. How can I get the moon for him?

**WISE MAN:** What you ask is impossible. Let your son be. He is young, and he will learn to get over this. As he grows older he will understand that there are some things he can never have. There are some things that are impossible to have. He will soon forget.

**KING:** But I will not forget. I want my son to have everything he wishes. Now he wishes for the moon, and I want him to have it. How can I get the moon for him?

**WISE MAN:** Your mind will not be changed?

**KING:** No. My son, the prince, wants the moon. He will have the moon!

**NARRATOR:** The wise man knew better than to argue with the king. He retreated into his hut and began to think. For five long days he thought and thought. Finally he emerged from his hut and approached the king.

**WISE MAN:** I have a plan. I have a plan that will get the moon for your son, the prince.

**KING:** What is your plan?

**PRINCE:** Yes, what is the plan that will get me the moon?

**WISE MAN:** All the warriors in the kingdom must work together. They must work for the next 10 years building a scaffold to the sky. It must be the highest scaffold in the world. It must reach all the way into the sky.

**PRINCE:** Is that all?

**WISE MAN:** No! At the end of the 10 years you will climb all the way to the very top of the scaffold. During the darkest part of the night the moon will pass directly over the scaffold. You can then reach out and pull the moon out of the sky.

**KING:** I am very pleased. Let the building of the scaffold begin.

**NARRATOR:** And so it was. All the warriors devoted their energies to the building of the prince's scaffold. For 10 years; for 10 long years, they worked on building the highest scaffold anyone had ever seen or that anyone had ever imagined. For 10 long years they worked. Finally they were done.

**KING:** The scaffold is complete.

**PRINCE:** Now, I will get the moon! My moon!

**NARRATOR:** The king and the prince and all the people of the village climbed to the very top of the scaffold. It was the darkest part of the night. And just as the wise man had told them, the moon began to pass over the scaffold. The king reached out to grab the moon.

**KING:** OUCH! The moon is very hot. It is too hot to pull out of the sky. I cannot get the moon for you, my prince.

**PRINCE:** Then I will get it. I am older now. I am wiser now. I am stronger now. I will get the moon myself. I have been waiting for a long time . . . for 10 years I have been waiting to get the moon. It is mine . . . . I will have it!

From *African Legends, Myths, and Folktales for Readers Theatre* by Anthony D. Fredericks. Westport, CT: Teacher Ideas Press. Copyright © 2008.

**NARRATOR:** The prince reached out to grab the moon. As he touched it, smoke began to curl from his fingers. He pulled even harder. As he did, flames shot out from his hands. Suddenly the moon began to break into many pieces. The pieces rained down on the people standing on the scaffold. The scaffold burst into white hot flames. The king, the prince, and all the people began to fall to the earth.

**KING:** Help us, help us, help us!

**PRINCE:** We will die! We will die! We will die!

**NARRATOR:** The gods of Africa were watching. They took pity on all the people of the village. After all, they were only humans and they did not know any better. So the gods of Africa caught all the people of the village in their hands. They caught them all before they fell to the earth. The gods let the people live, but to punish them for their foolishness, they turned all the people into monkeys.

Today when you go into the jungle you will see all the monkeys high in the trees. The people of the village never did make it all the way back to the earth. They all became monkeys. Indeed, all those monkeys are a warning to other people who would be foolish enough to take something from the sky and claim it as their own.

From *African Legends, Myths, and Folktales for Readers Theatre* by Anthony D. Fredericks. Westport, CT: Teacher Ideas Press. Copyright © 2008.

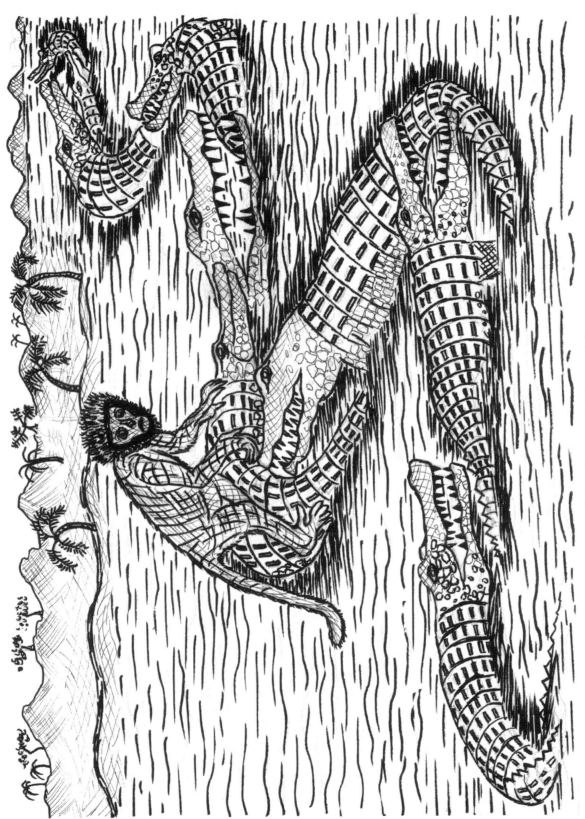

Monkey and Crocodiles

# Monkey and Crocodiles

## (Cameroon)

**STAGING:** The narrator may stand at a podium or lectern. The three crocodiles should stand in a straight line (each at a music stand or small table). The monkey may walk around among the other characters. You may wish to lay some blue ribbons on the floor to simulate a river.

---

|  |  |  |  |
|---|---|---|---|
| | Crocodile 1<br>X | Crocodile 2<br>X | Crocodile 3<br>X |
| Monkey<br>X | | | |
| Narrator<br>X | | | |

**NARRATOR:** Once upon a time, there was a small village. Near the village was a very wide river. The water in the river flowed swiftly. But on the other side of the river there was a banana plantation, rich with many bananas. It was said that the bananas were the best in all the land, and they were much prized. People from all over loved those bananas and would talk about them with much affection.

**MONKEY:** I, too, like those bananas. I would like to have some bananas to eat. They are very good, and I should like to have some for myself. I think I will go and get myself some excellent bananas.

**NARRATOR:** And so the monkey packed his bag and set out for the banana plantation. But first he came to the very wide river. He had to get across the river in order to get to the bananas he cherished so much. The river was very wide and very swift. And the monkey could not swim.

**MONKEY:** I do not know how to swim. How will I get across?

From *African Legends, Myths, and Folktales for Readers Theatre* by Anthony D. Fredericks. Westport, CT: Teacher Ideas Press. Copyright © 2008.

**NARRATOR:** The monkey sat down on the side of the river and thought and thought and thought. After a long time thinking, he came up with a plan . . . a very brilliant plan. He looked across the river and soon spied a crocodile swimming in the river.

**MONKEY:** Oh, my brother crocodile. You look very happy swimming in the river. I hope everything is good for you.

**CROCODILE 1:** Oh, yes it is. It is a very fine day, and I am a very happy crocodile.

**MONKEY:** I am so pleased to hear that my brother is happy today.

**CROCODILE 1:** Yes, I am. Perhaps you would like to join me. Perhaps you would like to swim with me, and we can enjoy this fine day together.

**NARRATOR:** But the monkey was a very wise monkey. He knew that if he even put his foot in the river the crocodile would immediately eat him up.

**MONKEY:** I would love to swim with you, my brother. But why should we have all the fun. Why don't we invite all your family?

**CROCODILE 1:** That is a very good idea, indeed.

**CROCODILE 2:** Yes, that is a very good idea. We should all swim together and enjoy this very fine day!

**CROCODILE 3:** Yes, I agree. It will be a great day all around.

**MONKEY:** That is so true, my brothers. But I am wondering how many there are of you. How many of your family are in this river? How many would I be swimming with?

**CROCODILE 2:** There are many of us.

**CROCODILE 3:** We are a very big family. A very big family indeed!

**CROCODILE 1:** We are such a large family that nobody can count all of us.

From *African Legends, Myths, and Folktales for Readers Theatre* by Anthony D. Fredericks. Westport, CT: Teacher Ideas Press. Copyright © 2008.

**MONKEY:** You may not believe me, but I can count. I can count very well. I will count all of you, and then we will know how many of you there are.

**CROCODILE 2:** Can you believe that? A monkey who can count!

**CROCODILE 3:** I don't believe it! I don't think a monkey can count.

**MONKEY:** It is true. I can count very well. Very well indeed!

**CROCODILE 1:** Well, then let us see for ourselves.

**ALL CROCODILES:** Brothers! Sisters! Come out! Come out!

**NARRATOR:** All the crocodiles poked their heads out of the water. They all looked at the monkey.

**MONKEY:** So that I may count all of you, you must line up from one bank of the river to the other. You must all be together from one side of the river to the other side. That is the only way I can count you. That is the only way to know how many of you there are.

**NARRATOR:** So all the crocodiles lined up. They lined up from one bank of the river to the other bank. Then the monkey started walking on the crocodiles' backs. As he walked, he started counting them.

**MONKEY:** [slowly moving in on top of the crocodiles] 1, 2, 3, 4, 5 . . . .

**NARRATOR:** When he was about halfway across the backs of the crocodiles, he nearly fell into the water.

**MONKEY:** Be still, my friends. I want to be sure to count each one of you.

**CROCODILE 1:** We will be still.

**CROCODILE 2:** Yes, we will not move.

**CROCODILE 3:** We want you to count each one of us.

**NARRATOR:** And so the monkey continued his count as he made his way across the backs of all the crocodiles.

**MONKEY:** 57, 58, 59, 60 . . . .

**NARRATOR:** Finally the monkey reached the last crocodile and was about to leap onto the other bank of the river.

**CROCODILE 1:** Wait! Get hold of the monkey.

**CROCODILE 2:** He is going to jump away.

**CROCODILE 3:** He is going to get across the river.

**NARRATOR:** But it was already too late. The monkey jumped from the back of the last crocodile onto the other river bank. He had succeeded in getting across the river.

**MONKEY:** Ha, ha, ha. My little plan worked. Good-bye, my brothers. Thank you for giving me a bridge across the wide river. Perhaps I shall see you again on another journey.

**ALL CROCODILES:** We've been tricked!

**NARRATOR:** And the monkey traveled to the banana plantation and had himself a great feast of delicious bananas.

**ALL CROCODILES:** We've been tricked!

**NARRATOR:** This story reminds us that you don't have to be big and strong to succeed in life. You just have to be a little bit smarter than others who would do you in.

From *African Legends, Myths, and Folktales for Readers Theatre* by Anthony D. Fredericks. Westport, CT: Teacher Ideas Press. Copyright © 2008.

The Guardian of the Pool

# The Guardian of the Pool

## (Central African Republic)

**STAGING:** The two narrators should be placed behind lecterns or podiums. The two characters should be free to walk around the staging area (with their scripts in their hands). They may wish to practice some simple movements (sitting down, looking upward, etc.) in concert with the evolving story.

---

|  | Ngosa<br>X | Python/Young Man<br>X |  |
|---|---|---|---|
| Narrator 1<br>X |  |  | Narrator 2<br>X |

**NARRATOR 1:** In a beautiful land in a faraway place there is a lovely lake. It is surrounded by lush green forests and towering cliffs.

**NARRATOR 2:** Beautiful flowers spill over the sides of the lake and down into the water. Colors swirl with the sunlight that dances across the surface of the lake.

**NARRATOR 1:** Green grasses grow beside the lake and cast their colors upon its surface. Clusters of flowering trees are sprinkled around the edges of the lake, filling the air with sweet scents.

**NARRATOR 2:** Big-winged butterflies flit over the lake in great swarms. Their wings are silent, but their beautiful colors cast shimmering hues upon the water.

**NARRATOR 1:** In the middle of the lake the waters swirl. They circle around and around, making a great whirlpool that glistens in the noonday sun.

**NARRATOR 2:** Red and gold leaves that fall from the trees overhead spin around and around in the whirlpool. It is a never-ending circle of color, a never-ending circle of beauty.

From *African Legends, Myths, and Folktales for Readers Theatre* by Anthony D. Fredericks. Westport, CT: Teacher Ideas Press. Copyright © 2008.

**NARRATOR 1:** At the very bottom of the whirlpool lies a wonderful silver water python. There is coil after coil—each layered one upon the other—each a silver circle that shines up through the ripples of the water.

**NARRATOR 2:** The python is the guardian of the pool . . . a silver guardian who lies at the bottom of the pool, his tongue flickering in and out of his silver mouth. He is not feared, but he is known.

**NARRATOR 1:** Is has been said across the land that this python, this guardian of the pool, has magical powers.

**NARRATOR 2:** It is said that this python, this guardian of the pool, has healing powers unlike any other creature.

**NARRATOR 1:** It is said that any who touch the skin of the python—the guardian of the pool—will be healed.

**NARRATOR 2:** It is said that any who touch the silver skin of the python—the guardian of the pool—will have all their illnesses disappear, all their pains whisked away, and all their aches eliminated.

**NARRATOR 1:** The guardian of the pool is a magical creature.

**NARRATOR 2:** The guardian of the pool is a wondrous creature.

**NARRATOR 1:** Now in that time there was a very beautiful girl. Her name was Ngosa, and her soft black hair shown in the sunlight. Her smooth brown skin glistened in the moonlight. Her eyes were like soft pools of water and her hands were filled with gentle warmth.

**NARRATOR 2:** But Ngosa was also sad. Her mother was very, very ill and had been so for a long time.

**NGOSA:** I must help my mother. Without my help she will surely die. I need to help her. And I know that the only way I can help her is if I touch the skin of the serpent who lies in the whirlpool. I must touch the guardian of the pool, the python with the silver skin.

**NARRATOR 1:** Ngosa was afraid. She was very afraid.

From *African Legends, Myths, and Folktales for Readers Theatre* by Anthony D. Fredericks. Westport, CT: Teacher Ideas Press. Copyright © 2008.

**NARRATOR 2:** But she also knew what she had to do. She shivered and she trembled.

**NGOSA:** I am so afraid. I am afraid for my mother. And I am afraid for myself. I know what I must do. For if not, then my mother will surely pass.

**NARRATOR 1:** There was fear in her heart.

**NARRATOR 2:** There was trembling in her soul.

**NGOSA:** I am afraid. But I also have many fond memories of my mother. I remember all the times I would listen to her lullabies, all the lullabies she would sing to me as a child. I remember all the times my mother would walk long miles to gather food to sustain me when I was young. I remember how my mother would travel over the countryside to gather medicines when I was sick or when I was stung by the lash of the scorpion's tail. I remember the great drought and how my mother begged and pleaded with every villager to get me water. I remember how she beat away the monkeys who came to steal what little food we had. I remember many things about my mother. I know I must do what I must do to save her.

**NARRATOR 1:** With that Ngosa stepped into the pool.

**NARRATOR 2:** The guardian of the pool—the silver python—waited in the depths of the pool.

**NARRATOR 1:** Ngosa swam, swam, swam to the bottom of the pool. Fear gripped her heart.

**NARRATOR 2:** She reached out—very carefully—she reached out and gently stroked the skin of the silver python.

**NARRATOR 1:** Then, kicking with all her strength, she rose to the surface of the pool.

**NARRATOR 2:** She raced across the fields and into the hut of her mother. She touched her mother with the python's healing touch. And her mother was well again.

From *African Legends, Myths, and Folktales for Readers Theatre* by Anthony D. Fredericks. Westport, CT: Teacher Ideas Press. Copyright © 2008.

**NARRATOR 1:** Later that night an orange-red moon rose over the valley. The guardian of the pool—the silver python—rose to the surface.

**NARRATOR 2:** Out of the water stepped a handsome young man. His head was covered with long black curls. His eyes were without fear and there was great strength in his arms. His long legs were swift and his chest was broad.

**NARRATOR 1:** He strode from the pool and across the ground. He soon came to the huts clustered beside a great mountain. He stood outside the first hut.

**PYTHON/YOUNG MAN:** Ngosa. Ngosa. You have shown great courage. You have shown great strength.

**NGOSA:** I do not know you. Who are you?

**YOUNG MAN:** I am the silver python. Long, long ago the Water Witch cast a spell upon me. I sank to the bottom of the pool and rested there long days and long nights. I was commanded to guard the whirlpool. But your courage, your strength, has changed me. Your touch has changed me back into my human form. By your courage I may assume my human form during the night. I may reveal my human form to those who are both brave and beautiful. You were brave to visit me. You were brave to touch me at the bottom of the pool. And you are also very beautiful.

**NGOSA:** I am so very happy. I am so very happy I have found you.

**YOUNG MAN:** Come here. I wish to give you something.

**NGOSA:** What is it? What is it you wish to give me?

**YOUNG MAN:** It is a necklace. It is a necklace of moonstones. It is a necklace of moonstones strung on a thread of silver moonlight.

From *African Legends, Myths, and Folktales for Readers Theatre* by Anthony D. Fredericks. Westport, CT: Teacher Ideas Press. Copyright © 2008.

**NARRATOR 1:** And now Ngosa spends all her days beside the whirlpool. She plays sweet music on a simple gourd. That is because the music of a gourd is the sweetest of sounds to a python.

**NARRATOR 2:** And each night Ngosa slips a beautiful necklace of moonstones around her neck. And she waits. She waits for a handsome young man to rise up out of the silver waters . . . as he does each night.

Shansa Mutongo Shina

# Shansa Mutongo Shima

## (Democratic Republic of the Congo)

**STAGING:** The characters and narrators should all be seated on tall stools or chairs. Their scripts should be placed on music stands or lecterns. The two narrators may be standing or seated on stools. They should be placed at opposite ends of the staging area

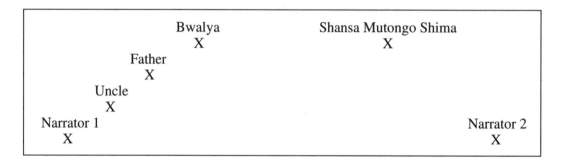

**NARRATOR 1:** This is a story from many years ago. Listen carefully to this story, for it has a lesson that is important for all, especially for the young ones.

**NARRATOR 2:** You see, deep in the forest there lived a very beautiful woman. Her name was Bwalya. Now this Bwalya was the most beautiful woman anyone had ever seen. Not only was she most beautiful, but she was very smart indeed. Because she was so beautiful and because she was so clever, many men from throughout the land came to court Bwalya. They would bring her many shells from deep in the sea. They would bring her the finest yams from faraway fields. They would offer her wonderful houses filled with treasures and fine gifts.

**NARRATOR 1:** But, you see, Bwalya did not find any of these suitors very interesting. She grew tired of all they had to offer. She grew tired of all they said to her. She decided that she did not want to marry any of them. So she sent all of them away.

 From *African Legends, Myths, and Folktales for Readers Theatre* by Anthony D. Fredericks. Westport, CT: Teacher Ideas Press. Copyright © 2008.

**NARRATOR 2:** Then one day there came a stranger from a distant place. He wore a top hat and was dressed in a fine suit. He carried a gold watch in his pocket. When he talked, everyone laughed. He had traveled to many places and had many stories to tell. Everyone enjoyed what he said, for he was very handsome and very clever.

**NARRATOR 1:** Now, as you quite well know from these stories, this stranger came to meet young Bwalya. She quickly fell in love with him. Many women told her that she should be very careful. After all, he was a stranger and nobody knew where he lived or how he made his living. All the women of the village cautioned Bwalya; although the stranger was very handsome, he was unknown to everyone.

**NARRATOR 2:** Well, there came the day when this handsome stranger asked to take Bwalya's hand in marriage. She quickly accepted and announced to all that she would become his wife.

**FATHER:** My beautiful daughter will marry the handsome man known as Shansa Mutongo Shima. There will be a feast. There will be dancing. There will be singing. There will be much joy in my family, and there will be much joy in the whole village.

**BWALYA:** I shall marry this handsome man. I shall take him as my husband, and I will have much joy in my life.

**NARRATOR 1:** Bwalya's father ordered a great feast. He said that there would be 10 days of feasting. He said that there would be 10 days of celebration before the wedding.

**NARRATOR 2:** On the first day of the feast, Shansa Mutongo Shima approached Bwalya's father.

**SHANSA:** Oh, kind one. I bring you food for your great feast. I have gone into the jungle, and I have killed many animals for the feast. There is much game, and I am happy to share all this game with the village. Eat. Enjoy. Celebrate.

**NARRATOR 1:** Everyone was very happy. Shansa Mutongo Shima had brought many game animals for the feast.

**NARRATOR 2:** Every day of the feast, Shansa Mutongo Shima would arrive with his arms filled with all sorts of game animals for the feast. Nobody knew how he did it. Many times hunters would go into the bush to hunt for game, and many times those hunters would return empty-handed.

**NARRATOR 1:** But every day Shansa Mutongo Shima would come into the village and deliver a great armload of game animals for the feast. The villagers did not know how he did this, how he was able to bring so much game into the village each and every day of the feast. They did not know, but they were very happy with so much meat . . . with so much food.

**NARRATOR 2:** They did not know . . . you see, they did not know that Shansa Mutongo Shima was a shape changer. They did not know that he could change his shape. They did not know that each day he would go out into the bush and take off his human skin. And when he did so, there was the form of a lion underneath.

**NARRATOR 1:** Yes, my friends, there was a lion underneath the shape of a man. And this lion would dance and sing, and all the animals would come out of the bush to dance and sing, too. They would dance so long that eventually they would drop dead from all the dancing.

**NARRATOR 2:** And then Shansa Mutongo Shima would gather all their bodies and take them back to the village for the great feast.

**BWALYA:** Oh, my husband to be, how is it that you are such a great hunter when the men of my village have much difficulty finding game?

**SHANSA:** I am a wise and clever hunter. I know all about the animals. I can catch anything that I want. I am a fine hunter . . . a fine hunter, indeed.

**BWALYA:** But how do you do it?

**SHANSA:** With cleverness. With great cleverness.

**NARRATOR 1:** But Bwalya was suspicious. So the next day she went into hiding. Soon Shansa Mutongo Shima came down the path. She saw him take off his human skin to reveal a lion underneath.

**NARRATOR 2:** Bwalya ran back to the village. She wanted to tell everyone what she had seen, but she knew that nobody would believe her. She knew that the villagers would not believe that this handsome man was actually a lion in disguise. So she thought and she thought.

**BWALYA:** Oh, father, tomorrow you must come with me on a walk. We have many things to talk about before the wedding.

**FATHER:** Very well. Let us go for a walk and talk.

**NARRATOR 1:** The next day the two of them walked down the path. As they rounded a corner, they both saw Shansa Mutongo Shima taking off his human skin to reveal the lion.

**NARRATOR 2:** The lion began to dance and sing. Bwalya and her father ran back to the village and sought out her uncle.

**FATHER:** You will not believe what we have just seen!

**UNCLE:** Please tell me. I want to know.

**FATHER:** It is a sight that you, in all your wisdom, would not believe.

**BWALYA:** Yes, oh wise uncle, it is a sight that very few have ever seen. Even an old man as wise as you has never seen such a sight.

From *African Legends, Myths, and Folktales for Readers Theatre* by Anthony D. Fredericks. Westport, CT: Teacher Ideas Press. Copyright © 2008.

**UNCLE:** Then I must see this sight.

**FATHER:** Then we shall go tomorrow to see.

**NARRATOR 1:** The next morning Bwalya, her father, and her uncle went down the path. As they rounded a corner they saw Shansa Mutongo Shima take off his human skin and appear as a lion. He began to dance and sing. And as he did the three of them ran back to the village.

**UNCLE:** We must kill him. He is evil and must die!

**BWALYA:** No, I have a much better plan.

**FATHER:** I hope it is a good one. Shansa Mutongo Shima is very clever. We must be more clever than he.

**BWALYA:** Do not worry, for I have a very clever plan.

**NARRATOR 2:** That night Bwalya, her father, and her uncle gathered together four leopard skins, six bamboo sticks, and a pair of antlers. They crept to the place where Shansa Mutongo Shima was sleeping.

**NARRATOR 1:** They each draped a leopard skin over their back. Bwalya's uncle climbed on the back of her father. Then Bwalya climbed onto her uncle's back. They each held bamboo sticks in their hands. They looked like an enormous creature.

**NARRATOR 2:** They began to wave their sticks and dance in the moonlight. Shansa Mutongo Shima woke up to see a very large creature dancing over the ground. The creature was large. The creature was angry. The creature was the scariest things that ever was.

**NARRATOR 1:** Shansa Mutongo Shima was very frightened. This was a creature he had never seen before. He did not know what to make of this creature with four legs, six arms, a large hump on its back, and long sharp antlers.

**NARRATOR 2:** The creature moved closer to Shansa Mutongo Shima. He became very frightened . . . so frightened, in fact, that he tore off his human skin and ran far into the darkness as fast as he could.

**BWALYA:** We have scared Shansa Mutongo Shima away.

**FATHER:** He will never fool us again.

**UNCLE:** We made a scary creature. But one not as scary as Shansa Mutongo Shima would have been as a husband for Bwalya.

**NARRATOR 1:** The three returned to the village. Bwalya soon met another man. This was an honest man and a very kind man. She fell in love and the two of them married.

**NARRATOR 2:** Over the years, Bwalya had many children, and her children had many children.. She was a very happy mother. And she was a very happy grandmother.

**NARRATOR 1:** And many times she would share the story of Shansa Mutongo Shima with her children and grandchildren.

**BWALYA:** Listen, my children. You must always pay attention to what lies inside a person. For what lies inside a person is much more important than what you might see on the outside. Take your time. Listen. Watch. Observe. Do these things before you make any final decision about a person. Do these things, and you shall always be happy.

**NARRATOR 2:** And they did these things. And they were always happy. And that is a lesson for us all.

From *African Legends, Myths, and Folktales for Readers Theatre* by Anthony D. Fredericks. Westport, CT: Teacher Ideas Press. Copyright © 2008.

# PART III
# NORTHERN AFRICA

# The Merchant of Tarbooshes

## (Tunisia)

**STAGING:** The characters should all be standing. They may wish to hold their scripts in their hands or place them on music stands.

---

| Narrator 1 | | Merchant | Thief 1 | Thief 2 | Narrator 2 |
|---|---|---|---|---|---|
| X | | X | X | X | X |

**NARRATOR 1:** Now once in a long ago time that there lived a merchant. He was a very wise merchant, and he traveled far and wide across the reaches of Tunisia to sell his wares.

**NARRATOR 2:** Now it should be said that his wares consisted entirely of tarbooshes.

**MERCHANT:** [to the audience] Yes, I am a merchant of tarbooshes. For those who may not be familiar with this traditional ware, allow me to explain. You see, a tarboosh is a hat worn by men. It has been worn for a very, very long time. It is one of the traditions of my country of Tunisia. The hat is very special. It is made from red felt and wool. And it is decorated with a tassel on the top. Many men wear tarbooshes, as is the custom and the tradition.

[to narrator 1] You may now carry on, my good friend. I am sure that my friends here [points to audience] wish to hear more of your wonderful story. Please proceed.

**NARRATOR 1:** [to the merchant] Thank you, most gracious one.

[to the audience] The merchant [points] traveled with his donkey over many miles to sell his tarbooshes to all who would want them. They were prized by many as some of the finest in all the land. The journeys from marketplace to marketplace were often very long and very tiring.

**NARRATOR 2:** And so it was that one day, the merchant became very tired from his travels.

**MERCHANT:** I shall lay down to sleep and to gather my strength, for I am very tired.

**NARRATOR 1:** And so the merchant slept peacefully in the shadow of a large tree. But what he didn't know was that the tree was filled with monkeys.

**NARRATOR 2:** As soon as the merchant fell asleep, the monkeys scampered down from the branches of the tree.

**NARRATOR 1:** The monkeys gathered up all the tarbooshes that were in the merchant's baskets. They quickly scampered up into the branches of the tree.

**NARRATOR 2:** Soon the merchant awoke from his nap. He discovered that all his baskets were empty. Looking around, he saw all the monkeys in the tree, each with a tarboosh on its head.

**MERCHANT:** COME HERE! COME HERE, you monkeys! You have my tarbooshes, and I want them back!

**NARRATOR 1:** But as you might imagine, the monkeys did not pay any attention to the merchant.

**NARRATOR 2:** They completely ignored the merchant. They paid no attention at all.

**MERCHANT:** COME HERE! COME HERE, you monkeys! You have my tarbooshes, and I want them back!

**NARRATOR 1:** He kept yelling and yelling. But each time he yelled, the monkeys yelled back at him.

**NARRATOR 2:** He stamped his feet over and over again. But each time he stamped his feet, the monkeys would stamp their feet, too.

**MERCHANT:** COME HERE! COME HERE, you monkeys! You have my tarbooshes, and I want them back!

**NARRATOR 1:** The merchant became very frustrated. Each time he said something and each time he did something, the monkeys would only mimic him.

**NARRATOR 2:** That's when our very wise merchant got an idea.

**MERCHANT:** COME HERE! COME HERE, you monkeys! You have my tarbooshes, and I want them back!

**NARRATOR 1:** But this time when he yelled at them, he threw his own hat on the ground.

**NARRATOR 2:** The monkeys saw what he did, and they all threw their hats to the ground.

**NARRATOR 1:** The very wise merchant gathered up all his tarbooshes and put them in his baskets and tied the baskets to his donkey. He had fooled the monkeys at their own game.

**NARRATOR 2:** He then set out on his journey once again. But this time he was grinning from ear to ear.

**NARRATOR 1:** However, he was soon to have another adventure.

**NARRATOR 2:** It was while he was on the road. He was singing to himself as he was riding his donkey. Then he heard a voice.

**THIEF 1:** Halt there.

**THIEF 2:** Halt there.

**MERCHANT:** Who goes there?

**THIEF 1:** We do. We are thieves, and we mean to take your donkey.

**THIEF 2:** Yes, we will take your donkey. It is a fine donkey and will bring us much money in the marketplace.

From *African Legends, Myths, and Folktales for Readers Theatre* by Anthony D. Fredericks. Westport, CT: Teacher Ideas Press. Copyright © 2008.

**MERCHANT:** You cannot take my donkey. It is all I have.

**THIEF 1:** Give us the donkey. We want your donkey.

**THIEF 2:** Yes, you will give us your donkey immediately.

**MERCHANT:** Do not take my donkey. If you try to take my donkey, I shall be forced to do as my father did. I don't want to do it, but I may have to. I don't want to be without my donkey.

**THIEF 1:** Okay, we will not take your precious donkey.

**THIEF 2:** We will leave now. But tell us. What did your father do?

**MERCHANT:** He bought another donkey!

From *African Legends, Myths, and Folktales for Readers Theatre* by Anthony D. Fredericks. Westport, CT: Teacher Ideas Press. Copyright © 2008.

# The Jackal and the Farmer

## (Algeria)

**STAGING:** The characters should all be behind music stands or lecterns. They may be seated on tall stools or chairs throughout the entire production. The narrator should be standing near the back of the staging area.

---

```
                                                      Narrator
                                                         X


   Farmer          Lion
     X               X
                            Jackal
                              X              Wife
                                              X
```

**NARRATOR:** Once there was a farmer who would leave his home early in the morning to plow his fields. Each day he took his two oxen with him to pull the plow. One day, a lion approached the farmer.

**LION:** Give me one of your two oxen. If you do not, I will kill you and I will kill your two oxen.

**NARRATOR:** The farmer was very afraid of the lion. So he unhooked one of his oxen and gave it to the lion. The lion carried the oxen off into the bushes. The farmer went home with his remaining ox. Just before he arrived home, he purchased another ox so that he would be able to plow again the following day.

The next day the farmer plowed from early in the morning until late in the afternoon. Just before he was ready to head home, the lion appeared once again.

From *African Legends, Myths, and Folktales for Readers Theatre* by Anthony D. Fredericks. Westport, CT: Teacher Ideas Press. Copyright © 2008.

**LION:** Give me one of your oxen. If you don't give me an ox, I will kill both of your oxen and you in the bargain. Is that what you wish?

**FARMER:** No, I do not wish that. Here, take my ox.

**NARRATOR:** The lion took one of the farmer's oxen. He dragged it away into the bushes, where he killed it. That evening, on his way home, the farmer purchased another ox so that he would be able to plow his field again the next day.

The next day the farmer plowed his field from early morning until late afternoon. Just as he was ready to go home, the lion once again appeared.

**LION:** Give me an ox. I want one of your oxen. If you do not, I will certainly kill you. And I will kill both of your oxen. There will be no way for your fields to be plowed.

**NARRATOR:** And so the farmer gave the lion one of his oxen. On his way home, as he had before, he bought another ox so that he would have a pair in the morning.

Now this went on for many days. But one evening, as the farmer was driving his single ox home along the road, he was approached by a jackal.

**JACKAL:** Oh, my farmer friend, I see that the lion is taking an ox from you every night. You begin the day with two oxen, yet you always end the day with a single ox. How does that happen?

**FARMER:** You see, every day when I am finished with my plowing, the lion comes along and demands one of my oxen. Now, he is big and strong and angry, and I dare not anger him. I know he will kill me if I do not do as he says. So I do the only thing I can: I give him one of my oxen.

**JACKAL:** That is true. But if you allow me to help you, I think we can get rid of the lion forever.

**FARMER:** What do you suggest?

From *African Legends, Myths, and Folktales for Readers Theatre* by Anthony D. Fredericks. Westport, CT: Teacher Ideas Press. Copyright © 2008.

**JACKAL:** If you promise to give me a sheep, I will make sure that the lion will never bother you again.

**FARMER:** I will gladly give you a sheep if you can make the lion go away forever.

**JACKAL:** Tomorrow, I will hide on the hill. Then I will disguise my voice and call out. I will ask who is speaking with you. You will tell me that it is only a block of wood—an asko—who is speaking with you. Make sure that you also have a hatchet at the ready. Do you understand what you are to do?

**FARMER:** I understand! I will do as you say.

**NARRATOR:** The next morning the farmer followed his usual routine. He walked to the field with his two oxen and began to plow, just as he had always done. Except this time he had hidden a hatchet in his robes.

At the end of the day, the lion approached him and asked him for one of his oxen. The lion threatened the farmer with death if he did not turn over an ox. Then from inside the hill a deep voice was heard.

**JACKAL:** Farmer, who is speaking with you?

**LION:** Where is that voice coming from? I am not familiar with that voice. It sounds like a god from the hills. It is very frightening and I am very scared.

**FARMER:** [to the voice] It is only an asko. It is only a block of wood. I am only speaking with a block of wood.

**JACKAL:** Then you must take your hatchet and split the block of wood.

**LION:** [to the farmer] Please be gentle. Please, I beg of you, only give me a gentle blow.

**NARRATOR:** The lion bowed his head. The farmer gripped the hatchet with all his might and hit the lion over the head as hard as he possibly could. He hit the lion with so much force that the lion was killed instantly.

From *African Legends, Myths, and Folktales for Readers Theatre* by Anthony D. Fredericks. Westport, CT: Teacher Ideas Press. Copyright © 2008.

**JACKAL:** [to the farmer] You have done what I told you. And I have done what I promised. The lion is no longer a threat to you. Tomorrow I will return and claim the sheep you have promised me.

**FARMER:** And it shall be yours.

**NARRATOR:** And so the farmer returned home. Only this time he had both oxen with him. As he walked into his house, he spoke to his wife.

**FARMER:** The jackal has helped me. The jackal has freed me from the lion. Now I will give him a sheep. I will need to kill a sheep first and then you can pack it for me so that I can take it to the field tomorrow.

**WIFE:** Why shouldn't we eat the sheep ourselves? Why should we give the sheep to the jackal?

**FARMER:** You are right, good woman. What do you suggest?

**WIFE:** I suggest that you get our finest sheep. Kill the sheep and put it into a leather sack. Then put the leather sack into a basket. Then take the basket with you.

**FARMER:** Is that all?

**WIFE:** No, there is one more thing you must do.

**FARMER:** What is that?

**WIFE:** You must have our trusted dog lie down in the basket beside the sheep. But do not tell the jackal about the dog.

**NARRATOR:** And so it was that the farmer set out the next day with his two oxen and the basket. Inside the basket was the sheep and the family dog. When the farmer reached the field, he set down the basket and called out to the jackal.

**FARMER:** Oh, jackal, here is the sheep I promised you. Please claim your reward for helping me.

**NARRATOR:** The jackal slowly approached the basket in order to take the sheep. He stuck his nose inside the basket. Up sprang the dog, barking loudly. The jackal ran away as fast as he could. The dog chased after him for many miles, but eventually gave up and returned home.

**JACKAL:** The farmer tricked me. I will never again offer to help men. They are very tricky creatures indeed.

**NARRATOR:** The farmer picked up the basket and began to walk home. He walked into his house and spoke to his wife.

**FARMER:** You were right. The jackal has been scared away by our dog. Our finest sheep was left in the basket. Now we must celebrate, for we have tricked the jackal and we have a fine feast to prove it.

**NARRATOR:** And so the farmer and his wife ate until their bellies were full. And they were never bothered by a lion or a jackal ever again.

From *African Legends, Myths, and Folktales for Readers Theatre* by Anthony D. Fredericks. Westport, CT: Teacher Ideas Press. Copyright © 2008.

The Clever Snake Charmer

# The Clever Snake Charmer

## (Morocco)

**STAGING:** The characters may all be seated on chairs or stools. Their scripts should be placed on music stands, and they should be encouraged to use their arms and hands as each of them speaks.

---

| | Sultan | Selham | Executioner | |
|---|---|---|---|---|
| | X | X | X | |
| | | | | Narrator |
| | | | | X |

**NARRATOR:** It was very long ago when Morocco was ruled by Jadi, a sultan who was always bored. The days were long and hot, just as they are today, so the sultan always sought some type of entertainment to wile away his long hours. Each day he would call for an entertainer to amuse him.

One day he called for his fiddler to play him a tune. The fiddler was very good and played many songs to entertain the sultan. But eventually the sultan became bored with the music and ordered the unlucky fellow's head to be chopped off.

**EXECUTIONER:** [using chopping hand motions] Chop, chop, chop.

**NARRATOR:** After that he wished for more entertainment. So he called up his harp player. The harp player, also an accomplished musician, played many songs to entertain the easily bored sultan. But unfortunately, the sultan ran out of patience. And once again he ordered the executioner to chop off his head.

**EXECUTIONER:** [using chopping hand motions] Chop, chop, chop.

**NARRATOR:** The next day, the sultan ordered dancers to entertain him. But, alas, after an hour or so he became very bored with all the dancing and ordered all their heads to be chopped off.

**EXECUTIONER:** [using chopping hand motions] Chop, chop, chop. Chop, chop, chop. Chop, chop, chop.

**NARRATOR:** The situation was very bad. Everyone feared for their lives. It didn't make any difference whether one was an entertainer, a goldsmith, or a shop owner, everyone knew that one day they would be called to the sultan's palace to entertain him in some way. And they also knew that he would get bored and have their heads chopped off.

**EXECUTIONER:** [using chopping hand motions] Chop, chop, chop.

**NARRATOR:** Fear gripped the countryside. Chopped heads were all over the place. People fled to faraway lands. Nobody wanted to be close to the palace and the head-chopping sultan.

**EXECUTIONER:** [using chopping hand motions] Chop, chop, chop.

**NARRATOR:** Then one day Selham, the snake charmer, arrived at the palace.

**SELHAM:** I would like to entertain the sultan.

**NARRATOR:** He was taken to the sultan, who ordered him to play his flute. The snake charmer played his flute, and his snakes slithered out of their sack and around his legs. But before too long, the sultan became very bored.

**SULTAN:** Off, off with your head. I've had enough of you and your snakes.

**EXECUTIONER:** [using chopping hand motions] Chop, chop, chop.

**SELHAM:** Oh, most merciful sultan, perhaps it should be so. But, I would like one more chance. If you will give me one more chance, I believe I can make it worth your while.

**SULTAN:** Well, I believe a man should have one more chance. Let it be so. I will give you your chance tomorrow at noon. You must first arrive at the palace as both a rider and a pedestrian, both at the same time. That is my order. If you do not obey my order, you shall be turned over to my executioner, who will separate your head from your body.

**EXECUTIONER:** [using chopping hand motions] Chop, chop, chop.

**NARRATOR:** Selham bowed and left the palace. At noon the next day, the sultan stood on a terrace overlooking the gates to the palace. As the gates opened, he saw Selham coming through on the back of the smallest donkey he had ever seen. The donkey was so small that Selham's feet touched the ground on both sides. He was riding the donkey and walking at the same time.

**SULTAN:** Oh, I see that you are a very clever man. You have arrived as both a rider and a pedestrian. But you are not quite finished. So that you might spare yourself from the sword of the executioner . . . .

**EXECUTIONER:** [using chopping hand motions] Chop, chop, chop.

**SULTAN:** I must ask you three questions. If you do not answer the three questions correctly, then it's . . . .

**EXECUTIONER:** [using chopping hand motions] Chop, chop, chop.

**SELHAM:** Very well, your majesty. I am ready for your three questions.

**SULTAN:** Good. Here is the first. How many stars are there in the sky?

**SELHAM:** Your majesty, the answer is quite clear. There are as many stars in the sky as there are hairs on my donkey, except for his tail. Would you like to count them yourself?

**SULTAN:** No, that is not necessary. Well, then, here's your second question. Tell me the part of the earth on which we are standing.

**SELHAM:** That should be quite obvious to a man of your infinite wisdom. We are standing in the middle.

**SULTAN:** Very good. You are indeed as wise as your name. But here is the third and final question. How many hairs are there in my beard?

**SELHAM:** Why, your most highest excellency, there are as many hairs in your beard as there are on the tail of my donkey. Perhaps you would like to cut off your beard and I will cut off my donkey's tail, and we can both count the hairs together.

**SULTAN:** That will not be necessary. You have indeed proved yourself to be a very clever man. It seems as though there is not a question that you cannot answer.

**NARRATOR:** It was then that the sultan summoned one of his attendants to fetch a bag of gold coins. The sultan presented the snake charmer with the bag and sent him on his way. The snake charmer slowly rode away on the back of his donkey. There was a big smile on his face . . . because he knew how to keep his head.

**EXECUTIONER:** [using chopping hand motions] Chop, chop, chop.

A Most Wise Baker

# A Most Wise Baker

## (Egypt)

**STAGING:** All five narrators can be standing or seated on tall stools. They may wish to hold their scripts in their hands or place them on music stands. Since there are no characters for this production, each of the narrators should be encouraged to speak with emotion and animation.

---

| Narrator 1 | Narrator 2 | Narrator 3 | Narrator 4 | Narrator 5 |
|:---:|:---:|:---:|:---:|:---:|
| X | X | X | X | X |

**NARRATOR 1:** This is not an ancient story, but one that occurred in more recent days.

**NARRATOR 2:** It is a story of a baker, a man with the name of Fathi. He was a very famous baker, and his bread was known far and wide—throughout all of Egypt—as the finest bread to be eaten anywhere.

**NARRATOR 3:** But it is also a story about his nephew—Samir— who was apprenticed to Fathi. Samir learned all he could about making bread. He learned about the right temperature for the ovens. He learned about the proper placement of the ingredients. And he learned about the very precise mixture of those special ingredients.

**NARRATOR 4:** Samir was a hard-working boy. He would often rise at 4:00 in the morning to begin his tasks. Not only did he have to learn about the baking of the bread, but he also had to pack and load and deliver the bread to all the customers—far and wide—who ate the very special bread made by his uncle Fathi.

**NARRATOR 5:** Fathi was a very demanding uncle. He wanted Samir to learn everything there was to learn about baking bread. But he also wanted Samir to learn about how to take care of the customers who came into the little shop to purchase the bread. There was always much to do. And there was always much to learn.

**NARRATOR 1:** Each morning the old man and the young man would begin to prepare the dough to be baked in the ovens.

**NARRATOR 2:** Fathi would carefully blend the ingredients together.

**NARRATOR 3:** He would carefully fold the mixture with his hands until it was the right consistency.

**NARRATOR 4:** All the time he was mixing and folding, young Samir would read the newspaper to Fathi.

**NARRATOR 5:** That was because the uncle, in learning all he could about his craft, had never learned how to read. He had left school to become a baker, and a most famous baker at that.

**NARRATOR 1:** But in taking all the time to learn about baking bread, Fathi had never taken the time to learn to read.

**NARRATOR 2:** So young Samir read the newspaper to his uncle every morning. Every morning, as the uncle was preparing his loaves of bread, young Samir would read the newspaper.

**NARRATOR 3:** This was a special time for both the uncle and his young nephew. Fathi would learn all about his neighbors as well as people in faraway places.

**NARRATOR 4:** Young Samir would have this special time with his uncle. He would carefully watch his uncle mix the bread dough. And he would have some valuable time with his uncle discussing the events of the day—both near and far.

**NARRATOR 5:** The uncle and his nephew would partake of their morning meal together. They would enjoy a large pot of tea, a loaf of bread, and much good conversation. It was a very special time for the two of them.

From *African Legends, Myths, and Folktales for Readers Theatre* by Anthony D. Fredericks. Westport, CT: Teacher Ideas Press. Copyright © 2008.

**NARRATOR 1:** But one day while they were eating and reading and baking, something very wonderful happened.

**NARRATOR 3:** As Fathi opened the shop, there were two men waiting on the sidewalk. They were both dressed in white and looked very important.

**NARRATOR 5:** As they walked into the shop, they introduced themselves as representatives of three very large hotels in Cairo. They had heard many good things about the special breads that came out of Fathi's shop.

**NARRATOR 2:** They talked to Fathi and told him that they would like him to supply their three hotels with all the bread that they needed. And they wanted the bread to be delivered beginning the next morning!

**NARRATOR 4:** Papers were signed, and Fathi and his nephew quickly disappeared into the shop to begin their preparations. There was much to do—bread to be baked, boxes to be packed, and bread to be loaded.

**NARRATOR 3:** And there were many regular customers in the shop who had to be provided with the famous bread that Fathi baked.

**NARRATOR 5:** All through the day Fathi mixed and mixed and mixed. He baked many loaves of bread—adding the special ingredients as he had always done.

**NARRATOR 2:** Samir helped each of the customers who came to the shop for their special loaves of bread. He also helped his uncle mix the bread dough and load it into the ovens.

**NARRATOR 4:** It was a very busy day—much busier than usual. There were all the regular customers to serve, and now there were the three hotels that wanted the special bread of uncle Fathi.

**NARRATOR 1:** Into the night they both worked. Finally, with the moon high in the sky, they shut down the ovens and closed the shop. Both were tired. Both were weary.

From *African Legends, Myths, and Folktales for Readers Theatre* by Anthony D. Fredericks. Westport, CT: Teacher Ideas Press. Copyright © 2008.

**NARRATOR 4:** The next morning, as Samir opened the doors to the bakery, a large wagon rumbled down the street.

**NARRATOR 3:** Several men jumped out of the wagon and walked into the bakery. They began to grab the boxes of bread that Samir and Fathi had baked the previous day.

**NARRATOR 2:** They began to load the bread onto the wagon to transport it to the three hotels. Fathi and Samir helped them load the bread.

**NARRATOR 1:** When they were done, the men drove off in the wagon. Both Samir and Fathi sat down on tall stools and rested, for they were very tired from all their labors the day before.

**NARRATOR 5:** By then, the regular customers had begun arriving in the shop. They were all curious to know about the large wagon and how the three hotels had ordered Fathi's special bread.

**NARRATOR 3:** It was on the following day that a reporter came to the bakery. He talked to Fathi and he talked to Samir.

**NARRATOR 2:** He wrote a special story about the baker and his nephew and put it in the newspaper.

**NARRATOR 5:** Everyone far and wide read the story. Fathi and Samir became heroes. Everybody talked about them. Of course everybody learned about Fathi's bread and wanted to have some of his bread for themselves.

**NARRATOR 1:** People came to the bakery from miles around. Scores of people arrived—each one wanting a loaf of Fathi's bread.

**NARRATOR 4:** People walked great distances to get a taste of Fathi's bread. Dozens and dozens of people spilled out of the bakery and across the street. People were everywhere.

From *African Legends, Myths, and Folktales for Readers Theatre* by Anthony D. Fredericks. Westport, CT: Teacher Ideas Press. Copyright © 2008.

**NARRATOR 3:** The coffee shop next door served coffee and tea.

**NARRATOR 2:** Sandwiches were served, and there was much noise and there was much excitement.

**NARRATOR 5:** Because of all the food around, there was soon a swarm of flies. Flies began buzzing the people. Flies began buzzing through the bakery. Flies began buzzing all through the street.

**NARRATOR 4:** One of the flies landed on the nose of the barber's wife.

**NARRATOR 2:** Samir tried to shoo the fly away. But he was a little too hasty. He swatted the fly right against the nose of the barber's wife. The fly was smashed on her nose.

**NARRATOR 3:** The woman screamed and screamed and ran out into the street.

**NARRATOR 5:** Everyone was laughing. Everyone was laughing—except for the barber.

**NARRATOR 4:** He yelled at Samir. He told Samir that he would call the newspaper and tell them that there were flies all through the bakery. When everyone heard about the flies in Fathi's bakery, no one would want to buy the baker's bread, especially the three big hotels in Cairo.

**NARRATOR 2:** Fathi did not know what to do. His whole reputation was at stake. This was terrible. This was very, very terrible.

**NARRATOR 3:** Suddenly the owner of the coffee shop next door had a wonderful idea. He talked to Fathi. He talked to Samir.

**NARRATOR 1:** In the evening Samir walked to the house of the barber. There was a large tray on his head.

**NARRATOR 2:** The tray was covered by a pure white cloth of embroidered linen.

**NARRATOR 3:** When Samir got to the door of the barber's house, he knocked very gently. The barber opened the door and looked very angry.

**NARRATOR 4:** But Samir just lifted up the embroidered cloth to reveal a very large loaf of bread. The bread was decorated with sesame seeds. It had been made especially for the barber and his wife.

**NARRATOR 5:** The barber smiled at Samir and invited him into the house. Samir was asked to sit at the table. And there he enjoyed the finest loaf of bread that his uncle had ever baked. It was a loaf that would be talked about for days to come.

From *African Legends, Myths, and Folktales for Readers Theatre* by Anthony D. Fredericks. Westport, CT: Teacher Ideas Press. Copyright © 2008.

# PART IV
# SOUTHERN AFRICA

The Hare and the Hyena

# The Hare and the Hyena

## (Botswana)

**STAGING:** All the characters should be seated on tall stools or chairs. The narrator should be placed near the front of the staging area.

---

```
          Hare        Hyena
           X            X

                                 Lightning-Bird      Spider
                                       X               X
    Narrator
       X
```

**NARRATOR:** It was a long time ago when this story was told. It was in the days when animals could talk with one another and would behave often as humans would. In these days there were two rivals, the hare and the hyena. Although they were friends, they each tried to outdo the other. They would argue long into the night, each trying to prove that he was stronger or the wiser than the other.

**HARE:** I am far better than you, my friend. I am swift and can outrun any animal there is. I can outrun the fires that sweep across the land in the dry season.

**HYENA:** That may be so, my friend, but I certainly have more brains than you. Is it not so that all the animals come to me for special medicine when the grasses are dry and the danger of fire is high?

**HARE:** Perhaps that is so, but just because you have some herbs and medicines does not make you the smartest creature in the land.

**HYENA:** That may be your point, but I do not see any animals coming to you for advice. Surely they must know who is the wisest and smartest of all the creatures.

From *African Legends, Myths, and Folktales for Readers Theatre* by Anthony D. Fredericks. Westport, CT: Teacher Ideas Press. Copyright © 2008.

**HARE:** Well then, it seems that we should have a test to see who is the wisest and strongest animal in all the land. We will dig a pit and at the bottom we can create a hiding place—a place that will protect us. Then we will build a fire at the bottom of the hole and we shall each, in turn, spend the night in a special retreat. It is there that we shall test our special fire medicine. The one who survives the fire without harm must certainly have the greater power.

**HYENA:** Then let us make it so.

**NARRATOR:** So the two animals dug a great pit into the ground. Each one made a special hiding place for himself according to his species' custom. The hyena, according to his habit, dug a shallow cave in the dirt. The hare, as was his custom, dug a long and winding tunnel in the ground. When each was satisfied with his hole, they gathered a large amount of wood and placed it in the bottom of the hole.

**HARE:** My good friend, as you have said many times, you are the older of us two. Therefore, since I am the least important, I should go into the hole first.

**NARRATOR:** So it was that the hare sat at the entrance to his tunnel. The hyena lit the fire and jumped out of the way. As soon as the smoke rose into the air, the hare climbed all the way down to the bottom of his secret tunnel—a place where the flames and the heat could not reach him. Soon he rushed to the opening and called out.

**HARE:** Oh, my friend, I am burning!

**HYENA:** Stand on your head.

**HARE:** I am still burning.

**HYENA:** Then sit down!

**HARE:** I am still burning!

**HYENA:** Then stand up!

From *African Legends, Myths, and Folktales for Readers Theatre* by Anthony D. Fredericks. Westport, CT: Teacher Ideas Press. Copyright © 2008.

**HARE:** I am still burning!

**HYENA:** Then lie on your side!

**NARRATOR:** There was a long silence. When the fire burned away, the hyena looked down into the pit and saw no sign of the hare. He went home giggling and laughing because he thought that his rival had lost his life in the fire. However, the next morning when he returned to clear away the ashes, he was surprised to see the hare sitting at the edge of the pit.

**HARE:** Well, I had a very warm experience, but I think that my medicine protected me. Come, my friend, I believe that it is now your turn to show the power of your medicine.

**NARRATOR:** And so the two creatures placed a large bundle of wood at the bottom of the pit. They lit the fire and the hyena crawled into his shallow hole at the entrance to the pit. The hare hopped off to the side and watched the fire grow higher and higher. Soon the hyena called out to his old rival.

**HYENA:** Oh, my friend, I am burning!

**HARE:** Then stand on your head!

**HYENA:** I am still burning!

**HARE:** Then sit down!

**HYENA:** I am still burning!

**HARE:** Try standing up!

**HYENA:** Standing up is worse than sitting down!

**HARE:** Then do as I did. Lie down on your side!

**NARRATOR:** There was a loud scream, then silence. Hare went home, knowing that he had finally fooled his old rival. When he returned the next morning he found the body of the hyena stuck in his shallow hole in the ground. He then cut off one of the hyena's ears and made it into a whistle. He walked around

 From *African Legends, Myths, and Folktales for Readers Theatre* by Anthony D. Fredericks. Westport, CT: Teacher Ideas Press. Copyright © 2008.

everywhere playing his new musical instrument. All the animals came to listen to the wondrous music that the hare made.

**HARE:** I am the greatest! Look, everyone, I have the ear of my old rival, the hyena, and the sound that I can make with this ear proves that I am the wisest and most clever animal in all the land. You would do well to listen to my music. I am smarter than you can ever imagine.

**NARRATOR:** The sound of the ear-whistle reached up into the skies. It was there that the lightning-bird heard it. He swooped down to talk with hare.

**LIGHTNING-BIRD:** I hear your music. It is very beautiful. I would like to make such music myself. Please lend me your whistle so that I may fill the skies with such beautiful music.

**HARE:** What do you say? If I gave you my whistle, you might steal it from me and fly away, never to return. I would never be able to get it back.

**LIGHTNING-BIRD:** That is not so. I only wish to make beautiful music, as you do. I will stay by your side as I make the music and you can listen too. I will not take away your wonderful whistle.

**HARE:** Very well. Here, you may have my beautiful whistle.

**NARRATOR:** But the lightning-bird was not an honest creature. As soon as he had the whistle in his beak, he flew up into the sky and flew away from hare. He made music as he flew, but he had no intention of ever returning the beautiful whistle to its rightful owner.

**HARE:** Come back! Come back!

**NARRATOR:** But the lightning-bird would not return. The hare was very angry at himself. He was very sad because he did not know how he would ever get the whistle back from the lightning-bird. Finally he decided to ask an old friend, the spider, for his advice.

**SPIDER:** I can weave a special bag around you with my silk. Then I can pull you up into the sky, where you can take the whistle away from the lightning-bird.

**NARRATOR:** And so the spider began to weave his silk around and around the hare. When he was done, he threw a strand of silk into the wind and was carried aloft by the wind, up and up and up to a high cloud. Once on the cloud he carefully pulled on the length of silk he had tied to the hare. Soon the hare rose up to the sky. When he was high enough, he stepped out onto the cloud next to his friend, the spider.

**LIGHTNING-BIRD:** I cannot believe what I am seeing. I cannot believe that the hare has learned how to fly. He must be a very clever creature, indeed. I must give him back his whistle, for he is the cleverest animal of all!

**NARRATOR:** The lightning-bird handed the whistle back to the hare. Then the spider slowly lowered the hare down to the ground. All the other animals watched with amazement as the hare slowly came to rest on the ground. They had never seen anything like it before. They, too, were sure that the hare was possessed of a great magic.

**HARE:** So you see, my friends, I am the wisest of all creatures. Not even the great lightning-bird can escape me. There is no animal that is a match for my wits. I am the wisest of all.

**NARRATOR:** And so it was that the hare was considered to be the wisest of all creatures. And he was forever indebted to his friend, spider, for helping him prove his wiseness to all the creatures. And from that time forward to today, the hare and the spider have always been the best of friends. Their friendship has lasted throughout the ages and has continued to this day.

 From *African Legends, Myths, and Folktales for Readers Theatre* by Anthony D. Fredericks. Westport, CT: Teacher Ideas Press. Copyright © 2008.

Little Girl and the Monster

# Little Girl and the Monster

## (Lesotho)

**STAGING:** The two main characters (little girl, monster) should be seated on tall stools or chairs. They may wish to simulate some of the movements described in the script. The two narrators should be standing at music stands or lecterns. They should speak in a cautionary way—after all, there is an important lesson in this story.

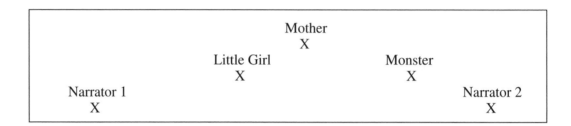

|  |  | Mother |  |  |
|  |  | X |  |  |
|  | Little Girl |  | Monster |  |
|  | X |  | X |  |
| Narrator 1 |  |  |  | Narrator 2 |
| X |  |  |  | X |

**NARRATOR 1:** A long, long time ago before any of the people now living were born, there lived a little girl.

**NARRATOR 2:** Now, this little girl thought that she was smarter than anyone. As a result, she did not always listen.

**NARRATOR 1:** There came a day when the little girl's mother called her and asked her to go out into the veldt to collect some roots and pick wild spinach to make a delicious stew.

**NARRATOR 2:** The little girl took her mother's basket and traveled a long way through the veldt. Finally she found a place where there were many wild roots.

**NARRATOR 1:** She began to dig in the ground. She placed all the uncovered roots into her basket.

**NARRATOR 2:** Now there is one thing we have not told you. We have not told you about the ugly monster that lived in the veldt. It was very ugly and it liked to eat humans.

**NARRATOR 1:** It was as tall as a tree and had teeth longer than those of a wild boar.

**NARRATOR 2:** But it especially liked to eat humans. Humans were very tasty treats for this large and very ugly monster.

**MONSTER:** Hey, little girl, I see that you are digging. I see that you are digging for roots in the earth. Is that not true?

**NARRATOR 1:** Now, you will remember that this little girl thought she was smarter than anyone. She thought she was better than anyone.

**NARRATOR 2:** And so she did not reply. She did not say anything to the large, ugly monster.

**MONSTER:** Hey, little girl, I can see that you are digging in the ground. I can see that you are digging for roots in the ground.

**NARRATOR 1:** This time the little girl decided to answer.

**NARRATOR 2:** This time the little girl decided to speak to the large and ugly monster.

**LITTLE GIRL:** You are right, you large and ugly monster. I am digging up all the roots that belong to the monster. I am picking all the spinach leaves that belong to the large and ugly monster. I am getting all this food to take back to my family. Ha, ha, ha!

**NARRATOR 1:** The monster was now angry. The monster walked toward the little girl in long strides. He wanted to catch her and eat her.

**NARRATOR 2:** But she was fast—like a field mouse. She ran away from him and slipped into a hole in the ground.

**NARRATOR 1:** The hole was just large enough for the little girl.

**NARRATOR 2:** But it was too small for the large and ugly monster.

**MONSTER:** Wait, you little girl. I am very smart. I will figure out a way to catch you. Then I will eat you. You will be very good to eat. You think you are smart, but I am smarter.

**NARRATOR 1:** The little girl laughed at the large and ugly monster. She called him many names. She made fun of him. She teased him and taunted him.

**LITTLE GIRL:** Monster, monster, go away. You are ugly every day! Monster, monster, go away. You are ugly every day!

**NARRATOR 2:** What the girl said hurt the ears of the monster. It felt as though there were fleas biting the insides of his ears.

**NARRATOR 1:** He could not bear to hear the little girl any longer.

**NARRATOR 2:** And so he walked home, and crawled into his hut.

**NARRATOR 1:** Soon after, the little girl crawled out from the hole. Seeing that the monster had gone away, she scuttled through the grass and traveled home.

**LITTLE GIRL:** I have brought many roots and many leaves for the stew.

**MOTHER:** Where did you get these, my child?

**LITTLE GIRL:** I had to go far away. I had to travel to the other end of the veldt. I had to travel to the land of the large and ugly monster.

**MOTHER:** Child, have I not told you to stay away from the monster? He will capture you and have you for supper. You will be a delicious treat for him.

**LITTLE GIRL:** I am not afraid, mother.

**MOTHER:** You should be afraid. He is very strong—like a bull. He is very dangerous—like a coiled snake.

**LITTLE GIRL:** But I am much smarter than he is. I am as clever as the jackal—perhaps even more so.

From *African Legends, Myths, and Folktales for Readers Theatre* by Anthony D. Fredericks. Westport, CT: Teacher Ideas Press. Copyright © 2008.

**MOTHER:** What are you saying? What are you saying?

**LITTLE GIRL:** I am saying that I am as clever as the jackal. I can hide in the ground. I can hide in the ground where the large and ugly monster cannot find me. Then, from inside the ground I can talk to the monster.

**MOTHER:** What do you say to him?

**LITTLE GIRL:** I say, "Monster, monster go away. You are ugly every day! Monster, monster, go away. You are ugly every day!"

**MOTHER:** What does the monster do then?

**LITTLE GIRL:** He is very angry. He stomps all over the ground, like a mad bull. He stomps, and stomps, and stomps.

**NARRATOR 2:** The mother warned her little girl again and again about the monster. But the little girl did not listen. She did not pay attention to her mother.

**NARRATOR 1:** So early the next morning the little girl took the basket and ran to the other end of the veldt. She ran to the place where the monster lived.

**NARRATOR 2:** She began to dig for roots. And she began to gather wild spinach leaves and put them into her basket.

**NARRATOR 1:** The large and ugly monster saw her.

**MONSTER:** There you are again. You are digging my roots. You are gathering my spinach.

**LITTLE GIRL:** Go away, you large and ugly monster. I am taking these roots and I am taking these spinach leaves for my family. Go away, monster.

**NARRATOR 2:** The monster chased after the little girl as fast as he could.

**NARRATOR 1:** But once again the little girl, as fast as a field mouse, scampered into a jackal's hole. She hid away from the reach of the monster.

**NARRATOR 2:** The monster was very angry. The monster was very furious. Once again, the little girl had escaped from him.

**NARRATOR 1:** But the little girl did not know something. She did not know that the monster was much more cunning than the jackal. She did not know that the monster was much smarter than any other animal on the veldt.

**NARRATOR 2:** So the monster sat outside the jackal's hole and waited for the little girl to come out.

**NARRATOR 1:** But the little girl was also cunning. But the little girl was also very smart. She waited—like a quiet field mouse—inside the hole.

**NARRATOR 2:** Then the monster had a clever plan.

**MONSTER:** Little girl, you must come out of the hole. Your mother is looking for you. She wants the roots you have gathered. She wants the spinach leaves you have picked. She is hungry and wants the food you have found.

**LITTLE GIRL:** I do not believe you. You are ugly. You are an ugly, ugly monster. Go away.

**NARRATOR 1:** The monster became very angry. He was so angry that he struck the ground with his fists.

**NARRATOR 2:** The little girl heard him strike the ground. But she did not care. She began to eats some of the roots. She began to eat some of the spinach leaves.

**NARRATOR 1:** Now the monster had another idea. He called to her in a high-pitched voice.

**MONSTER:** [in a high–pitched voice] Oh, my little girl. The sun is beginning to set and you must now come home.

**LITTLE GIRL:** You do not fool me, you large and ugly monster. You are still as ugly as an old baboon. You have teeth like a pig and a stomach like an old man.

**NARRATOR 2:** The monster listened and decided to make his voice even softer than before.

**MONSTER:** [softly] Little girl, little girl. The sun is now setting. It is time for you to come home.

**LITTLE GIRL:** Your voice sounds like rough rock. Your voice sounds like burnt trees. Your voice sounds like a dead hog. You are not my mother. Ha, ha, ha.

**NARRATOR 1:** The monster tried again in an even softer voice.

**MONSTER:** [much softer] Dear girl, I am waiting for my roots. I am waiting for my spinach leaves. Please come home.

**LITTLE GIRL:** You do not fool me. Your voice is still ugly. Your voice is still ugly—just as you are ugly. You cannot fool me.

**NARRATOR 2:** Finally the sun began to dip behind the hills to the west. The monster began to walk home.

**NARRATOR 2:** The little girl slipped out of her hole and ran all the way home to her mother.

**NARRATOR 1:** It is then that the monster had a brilliant idea. He ran back to the hole where the little girl always hid. He filled the hole with stones.

**NARRATOR 2:** But he left just enough room at the top for the little girl's head.

**NARRATOR 1:** The next morning the little girl skipped over the veldt to the place where roots grow and spinach leaves can be found.

**MONSTER:** Oh, I see that you have come again. I am hungry and will catch you and eat you up.

**LITTLE GIRL:** No, you won't. I am very clever and can always escape.

**NARRATOR 2:** The monster was very angry. He chased after the little girl.

From *African Legends, Myths, and Folktales for Readers Theatre* by Anthony D. Fredericks. Westport, CT: Teacher Ideas Press. Copyright © 2008.

**NARRATOR 1:** The little girl ran like a field mouse. She tried to slip into the jackal's hole.

**NARRATOR 2:** But because the monster had placed stones at the entrance of the hole, it was only the little girl's head that would fit into the hole. There was not enough room for the rest of her body.

**NARRATOR 1:** The little girl's body stuck out of the hole.

**MONSTER:** Ha, ha, ha. Look what I see! I see a little girl sticking out from the jackal's hole. Hmmm, she looks so delicious. And I am so hungry.

**NARRATOR 2:** And so the monster grabbed the little girl and put her into a bag.

**NARRATOR 1:** The little girl pleaded with the monster.

**LITTLE GIRL:** Let me out. Let me out. You must let me go! You must let me go!

**NARRATOR 2:** But the monster did not listen to her. He threw the bag over his shoulder and walked back to his home. He thought only of the delicious little girl he would eat.

**NARRATOR 1:** He thought only of the delicious little girl who would not listen to her mother.

**NARRATOR 2:** He would have a very good dinner.

**NARRATOR 1:** He would have a very good meal.

**NARRATOR 2:** And this is now the end of our story about a little girl who would not listen to her mother . . .

**NARRATOR 1:** . . . and a monster who was glad she didn't.

How the Tortoise Won Respect

# How the Tortoise Won Respect

## (South Africa)

**STAGING:** All the characters should be standing at lecterns or music stands. The story is told mainly by the four narrators. When the monster speaks, he should do so in a boastful, loud, and angry voice.

---

| Narrator 1 | Narrator 2 | Monster | Narrator 3 | Narrator 4 |
|:---:|:---:|:---:|:---:|:---:|
| X | X | X | X | X |

**NARRATOR 1:** It was the old days, a time long, long ago.

**NARRATOR 2:** It was in those days that the lion was the most powerful animal in the entire land. He was very mighty and he was very strong. His word was law and everyone obeyed him.

**NARRATOR 3:** Now in those days the animals did not have any food of their own. They were not yet good hunters. They had to sneak into the gardens of the humans and steal whatever vegetables they could.

**NARRATOR 4:** However, if they were ever caught by the humans, they ended up in someone's stewpot. Unfortunately, this happened far too often, and it worried the lion very much.

**NARRATOR 1:** So he called a meeting of all the animals.

**NARRATOR 2:** He told them that they must all move to another place.

**NARRATOR 3:** He told them that they must move to another place where there were no humans.

**NARRATOR 4:** He told them they must move to another place where they could plant their own food and live in peace.

**NARRATOR 1:** All the animals agreed with the lion.

**NARRATOR 2:** The cheetah was sent to steal some tools from the humans.

**NARRATOR 3:** The monkey was sent to steal some baskets from the humans.

**NARRATOR 4:** The rabbit was sent to steal some seeds from the humans.

**NARRATOR 1:** All the animals were sent off to search for a new place to live, a place where they could grow their own food.

**NARRATOR 2:** The faster animals—like the rabbit and the antelope—led the way.

**NARRATOR 3:** In the middle were the larger animals—like the buffalo, elephant, and giraffe.

**NARRATOR 4:** In the rear were the slower animals—like the tortoise and the chameleon.

**NARRATOR 1:** The animals traveled for a long time. Finally, the voice of the cheetah was heard from the front.

**NARRATOR 2:** The cheetah called out to everyone that he had found a beautiful place. It was a place, he said, where the land was very fertile.

**NARRATOR 3:** It was a place, the cheetah said, where there was a large lake filled with fresh water.

**NARRATOR 4:** It was a place, the cheetah said, where there were no humans to be found.

**NARRATOR 1:** The animals soon settled in. They worked very hard.

**NARRATOR 2:** They planted fields full of wonderful vegetables.

**NARRATOR 3:** The rains came and soon the fields were filled to overflowing with wonderful vegetables.

From *African Legends, Myths, and Folktales for Readers Theatre* by Anthony D. Fredericks. Westport, CT: Teacher Ideas Press. Copyright © 2008.

**NARRATOR 4:** There were large pumpkins, delicious carrots, great cabbages, and sweet, sweet potatoes.

**NARRATOR 1:** The animals could not believe their good fortune. Water was plentiful, food was plentiful, and their lives were very, very plentiful!

**NARRATOR 2:** But our story does not end there. For, as is the case in all stories, something will happen to the animals.

**NARRATOR 3:** And so it was.

**NARRATOR 4:** One day the animals awoke and set off for their garden. When they got there, they saw that every vegetable, every crop, everything they had planted was gone. There was nothing left.

**NARRATOR 1:** Even the lake was drained. There was not a drop of water to be found in the bottom of the lake.

**NARRATOR 2:** The animals could not believe what they were seeing. All that they had worked for, all that they had planted, was now gone.

**NARRATOR 3:** It was about this time that a very large and most enormous shadow fell across the sun.

**NARRATOR 4:** The sky went dark.

**NARRATOR 1:** There above them was a tremendous monster—a beast so large that it blotted out the sun.

**NARRATOR 2:** Its skin was gray and brown and smelled like the dung from dying warthogs.

**NARRATOR 3:** Its eyes were green and slimy.

**NARRATOR 4:** Its mouth was like a fantastic cave with rotting teeth and a breath that would kill forests of trees.

**MONSTER:** I AM THE MONSTER. I AM THE ONE WHO EATS ANIMALS WITH A SINGLE GULP. I AM THE ONE WHO OWNS THIS LAND. YOU ARE ON MY LAND. YOU ALL ANGER ME. I WILL EAT ALL OF YOU IN ONE SINGLE GULP!

 From *African Legends, Myths, and Folktales for Readers Theatre* by Anthony D. Fredericks. Westport, CT: Teacher Ideas Press. Copyright © 2008.

**NARRATOR 1:** The animals were terrified. They all ran back to their king, the lion. They all wanted to know what the lion would do.

**NARRATOR 2:** The lion told them not to be afraid.

**NARRATOR 3:** The lion told them that they should not be fearful.

**NARRATOR 4:** The lion told them that he would deal with the monster.

**NARRATOR 1:** And so the lion went to the field to confront the monster. But when he arrived he saw how very large this monster was.

**NARRATOR 2:** He realized that he did not have a chance of winning any fight against this monster.

**NARRATOR 3:** So he roared as loud as he could to scare away the monster.

**NARRATOR 4:** So he yelled as loud as he could to chase away the monster.

**MONSTER:** I AM THE MONSTER! THIS IS MY LAND. YOU ARE ON MY LAND. I WILL EAT YOU ALL. I WILL EAT YOU ALL WITH ONE LARGE GULP. YOU WILL ALL BE A MEAL FOR ME. I AM THE MONSTER AND I WILL EAT YOU!

**NARRATOR 1:** The monster scared the lion. He ran back to his hut with his tail between his legs. He thought that this monster was far more terrible than any of the humans he had seen.

**NARRATOR 2:** The other animals also thought that the monster was far too big and far too terrible to deal with. They, too, began to run away.

**NARRATOR 3:** But the tortoise decided otherwise. The tortoise announced that she was going to deal with the monster in her own way.

**NARRATOR 4:** The other animals laughed at the tortoise. They thought she was crazy to deal with such a large and fierce monster.

From *African Legends, Myths, and Folktales for Readers Theatre* by Anthony D. Fredericks. Westport, CT: Teacher Ideas Press. Copyright © 2008.

**NARRATOR 1:** But the tortoise was very wise and very clever. She asked the antelope to prepare a sharp ax for her. This he did, and she took the sharp ax and hid it under her shell.

**NARRATOR 2:** The tortoise, tiny and slow, walked up to the monster and shouted at him. She told him that she was tired of all his boasting.

**NARRATOR 3:** She told him that she was tired of all his bad breath.

**NARRATOR 4:** She told him that she was tired of all his smelly actions. And she told him to go away.

**MONSTER:** WHAT ARE YOU SAYING? DO YOU KNOW WHO I AM? I AM THE GREATEST CREATURE THERE IS. I CAN EAT ALL OF YOU IN ONE GULP. WHO IS THIS LITTLE ONE? I SHOULD HAVE HER FOR A SNACK. SHE WOULD TASTE VERY GOOD.

**NARRATOR 1:** And that is just exactly what the monster did.

**NARRATOR 2:** The monster swept up the little tortoise with his large smelly tongue.

**NARRATOR 3:** The little tortoise disappeared into the enormous mouth of the monster.

**NARRATOR 4:** As soon as the tortoise disappeared into the monster's mouth, she took the ax from under her shell. And, she began to chop at the monster's tongue.

**NARRATOR 1:** Chop, chop, chop!

**NARRATOR 2:** Chop, chop, chop!

**NARRATOR 3:** Chop, chop, chop!

**NARRATOR 4:** The monster cried out. He made loud sounds.

**MONSTER:** WHAT ARE YOU DOING? WHY DOES MY MOUTH HURT? YOU ARE HURTING ME. YOU MUST STOP! YOU MUST STOP, NOW!

From *African Legends, Myths, and Folktales for Readers Theatre* by Anthony D. Fredericks. Westport, CT: Teacher Ideas Press. Copyright © 2008.

**NARRATOR 1:** But the little tortoise did not stop.

**NARRATOR 2:** Chop, chop, chop!

**NARRATOR 3:** Chop, chop, chop!

**NARRATOR 4:** Chop, chop, chop!

**NARRATOR 1:** Finally the monster's tongue was chopped away from his mouth.

**NARRATOR 2:** The tortoise continued to swing her ax.

**NARRATOR 3:** She chopped across the neck of the monster.

**MONSTER:** ARRRR. ARRRR. ARRRR!

**NARRATOR 4:** Finally the monster fell to the ground. He was dead.

**NARRATOR 1:** The tortoise crawled out of the neck of the monster. She held her ax high in the air.

**NARRATOR 2:** All the animals cheered. All the animals cheered for the brave little tortoise, who had killed the very large and very ugly monster.

**NARRATOR 3:** All the animals called the brave little tortoise the cleverest animal of all.

**NARRATOR 4:** Even the mighty lion said that the tortoise was a very brave and very clever animal. And so it is to this day.

**NARRATOR 1:** She may be small.

**NARRATOR 2:** She may be slow.

**NARRATOR 3:** She may have a hard shell.

**NARRATOR 4:** But she is brave . . . very, very brave!

From *African Legends, Myths, and Folktales for Readers Theatre* by Anthony D. Fredericks. Westport, CT: Teacher Ideas Press. Copyright © 2008.

**Natiki**

# Natiki

## (South Africa)

**STAGING:** The narrator may be seated on a stool or chair in the front of the staging area. The other characters should be holding their scripts and are encouraged to walk around the staging area. You may wish to designate one part of the staging area as the dance area and another area as the mother's hut area. The characters can begin at the mother's hut, move to the dance area, and then move back to the mother's hut.

---

```
        Natiki          Mother
          X               X
                                  Sister 1
                                    X              Sister 2
                                                     X
     Hunter
       X
                                                            Narrator
                                                               X
```

**NARRATOR:** The sun was just setting over the land as all the hunters from the village returned for the evening meal. Women were preparing the food, and the children were playing games in the red-brown earth. There was much laughter and much talking all around.

**MOTHER:** Tonight is the Dance of the Full Moon. It is a night to celebrate. It is a night for much joy.

**SISTER 1:** Yes, we will dance and laugh.

**SISTER 2:** And we will eat and enjoy ourselves the whole night long.

**NARRATOR:** The three women began to prepare themselves for the big dance. Very carefully they began to rub their bodies with fat. Their skin glistened in the moonlight, making them seem beautiful and young.

But the youngest sister, Natiki, did not rub her body with fat.

**MOTHER:** Go, Natiki, go and fetch the goats. Make sure you bring all of them in before nightfall. Do not leave any goats out. They must all be here before the moon rises into the sky. Now hurry and go get them!

**SISTER 1:** Yes, go and get the goats, you stupid sister.

**SISTER 2:** Get them now. We can't be bothered. We are getting beautiful for the dance.

**MOTHER:** When you bring the goats, be sure to bring some wood for the fire. There should be a big fire to keep away all the large animals that prowl through the night. Get lots of wood so that the fire may burn all night long. Now go, my child. Do your chores and do them well. We must soon be off to the dance.

**NARRATOR:** Natiki was always treated badly by her mother and her sisters. They would always yell at her. They would always make her do all the work. They were always angry at her. It was said that Natiki was the most beautiful woman in the village, but her mother and two sisters never let her go out. Perhaps they were jealous. Perhaps they were very, very jealous.

**NATIKI:** I will do as my mother commands. I will do as my sisters ask. There is work to be done, and I will do it.

**NARRATOR:** Thus, Natiki went out to find the goats. She collected the wood. She had also gathered up a small bundle of porcupine quills, which she tucked into her clothing. When she finally returned to the hut, her mother and two sisters had already left for the dance. She put the goats into a pen and began to build a fire.

**NATIKI:** This is hard work. I am tired from all this work, but I would like to go to the dance. Perhaps I will meet a beautiful man there. Perhaps we will dance together in the night.

**NARRATOR:** Natiki began to rub melted fat all over her body. Her skin began to glow in the light of the moon. She brushed her hair and placed a necklace made from the shells of ostrich eggs around her neck. She threaded small beads through her hair. She was very beautiful indeed. Finally she placed the porcupine quills in a small pouch, which she tied around her waist.

**NATIKI:** It is time to go to the dance. It is time to have some fun.

**NARRATOR:** Natiki began to walk down a dusty path to the place where the dance was being held. As she walked, she stuck a porcupine quill into the dirt here and there. Soon she came to the top of a small hill and saw the dance off in the distance. There was much laughter and singing. The music was sweet and filled the night with joy. She moved on, and when she got to the fire she stood off to one side.

**MOTHER:** Who is that young girl? Have we seen her before?

**SISTER 1:** I do not know who she is. She must be a stranger.

**SISTER 2:** Yes, she must be new. She is very beautiful, but I do not know who she is.

**NARRATOR:** Soon Natiki moved to a group of women who were singing and clapping. She joined in the celebration, dancing and jumping with the others. She was filled with happiness and joy. Her steps were light and everyone noticed how well she moved around the fire. One person, a handsome hunter, could not take his eyes off Natiki.

**HUNTER:** She is the most beautiful woman I have ever seen. She dances like the wind. She laughs like a summer shower. She is so very beautiful!

**MOTHER:** I still do not know who that new woman is. She seems to have caught the eye of the handsome hunter.

**SISTER 1:** Yes, she is quite the dancer. She is very light on her feet.

**SISTER 2:** And her laughter is filled with much joy.

**MOTHER:** Oh, well. I think we are done here. Let us gather up some leftover meat and get on our way home. It is a long walk home, and we must be on our way.

**NARRATOR:** The mother and the two sisters started on their journey home. But, Natiki stayed and danced some more. Finally the handsome hunter approached her.

**HUNTER:** [to Natiki] You are a very beautiful dancer. You are like a gentle wind upon the savanna. I will walk you home.

**NATIKI:** Thank you. You are most kind.

**NARRATOR:** The hunter and Natiki followed the porcupine quills on the path home. As they walked, Natiki told the hunter about her family.

**NAKITI:** My mother and sister are mean. They treat me very badly. They make me do all the work and all the chores. All of the work falls to me. They are always angry with me.

**HUNTER:** Will they be angry with you tonight? Will they be angry because you came to the dance?

**NAKITI:** Yes, they will be very angry.

**HUNTER:** Then I will take you away from them. I will bring you to my house. I will make sure that there will always be meat in your pots and laughter in your house.

**NARRATOR:** As the hunter and Natiki approached, they were heard by the mother and two sisters.

**SISTER 1:** I wonder who that is. Whose are those two voices?

From *African Legends, Myths, and Folktales for Readers Theatre* by Anthony D. Fredericks. Westport, CT: Teacher Ideas Press. Copyright © 2008.

**SISTER 2:** Could it be our ugly sister and that young hunter? Why would he want to walk with her? She is so ugly.

**NARRATOR:** Just then Natiki and the young hunter appeared in the doorway. The glow from the fire shone on Natiki's skin. She looked very beautiful in the light. More beautiful than either sister.

**HUNTER:** I am taking Natiki away from this hut. I am taking her away for good.

**MOTHER:** What do you think you are doing? You can't take her away. She must stay here and do all our work. We need her here.

**HUNTER:** I am taking her away. She will become my bride, and I will make sure that her pots are full of meat and that our hut is filled with laughter.

**MOTHER:** Ha. You will see. She is no good. She must always be told. She must always be watched. She is useless!

**NAKITI:** I want to be with my new husband. I want to be away from here. This is what I want.

**NARRATOR:** And so the hunter and Natiki left the hut and went far away to the place of his own people. The hut where they lived was always filled with laughter. And Natiki's pots were always filled with meat. And soon they had many children and their lives were filled with much joy. Their life was very happy forever after.

From *African Legends, Myths, and Folktales for Readers Theatre* by Anthony D. Fredericks. Westport, CT: Teacher Ideas Press. Copyright © 2008.

# PART V

# WESTERN AFRICA

The Hunter and the Deer-Woman

# The Hunter and the Deer-Woman

## (Nigeria)

**STAGING:** All of the characters should be standing at music stands or lecterns. Most of the story is told by the three narrators, and the other characters may wish to interact with each other as appropriate.

---

|  | Narrator 1 | | Narrator 2 | | Narrator 3 | |
|---|---|---|---|---|---|---|
|  | X | | X | | X | |
| Hunter | | Deer-Woman | | Sister 1 | | Sister 2 |
| X | | X | | X | | X |

**NARRATOR 1:** These events happened a long time ago—long before any of us were around. But we shall tell them to you just as they were told to us, for we have no reason to do otherwise. You may wish to share them with others just as we are sharing them with you.

**NARRATOR 2:** There was once a hunter who came to rest by a swift river. As he was resting, he noticed a very beautiful woman bathing in the water. Her skin shone in the sunlight and her hair cascaded down over her shoulders like a waterfall. She was more beautiful than any woman he had ever seen.

**NARRATOR 3:** The hunter hid in the bushes so that she would not see him. As he did so, he saw a deer skin draped over a low branch. It was the color of bronze and was sprinkled with small dots. The fur was soft and velvety, and the hunter knew that this was the most perfect of all animal skins.

From *African Legends, Myths, and Folktales for Readers Theatre* by Anthony D. Fredericks. Westport, CT: Teacher Ideas Press. Copyright © 2008.

**HUNTER:** I have never seen a skin such as this. A skin like this would fetch a fine price at the market. It would fetch a price more than I could earn in an entire month's hunting.

**NARRATOR 1:** The woman climbed out of the water and ran across the grass. The hunter stood up and the woman saw him and stared. Her eyes were like bright coals, sparkling and shimmering in the sunlight. There was beauty all around her, and the hunter knew that he was looking at the most beautiful person in all the world.

**NARRATOR 2:** The hunter also knew that she was a deer-woman—a mysterious creature who roamed the ancient forests. Half-human and half-animal, they could change into either form at will.

**NARRATOR 3:** The hunter handed the deer skin to the woman, and she slowly began to walk away from him. His heart was sad as she moved into the nearby forest.

**HUNTER:** Stop! Please wait!

**NARRATOR 1:** The beautiful woman stopped and turned toward the hunter. Once again he saw a fire in her eyes. Once again he saw her soft bronzed skin. Once again he saw beauty all around her.

**HUNTER:** Please, please marry me. I beg of you, please marry me.

**DEER-WOMAN:** But you are a stranger. I do not know you. How can I marry someone I do not know?

**HUNTER:** I may be a stranger, but I am a man who loves you more than I love life itself. You are the most beautiful creature I have ever seen.

**DEER-WOMAN:** You must promise me one thing. You must promise that you will never tell any other human being the truth about me. If you do, I shall leave you forever. I will leave you forever and will never return.

From *African Legends, Myths, and Folktales for Readers Theatre* by Anthony D. Fredericks. Westport, CT: Teacher Ideas Press. Copyright © 2008.

**HUNTER:** I promise to keep your secret inside my heart. I promise never to tell another soul.

**NARRATOR 2:** The hunter and the deer-woman returned to the hunter's village. They were very happy together—indeed, they were the happiest two people in all the world. The hunter kept his promise—he never told anyone from where his new wife had come. Although many were curious, he kept the secret locked safely in his heart. Every day their love grew stronger and every day they both were happier.

**NARRATOR 3:** But there is more that we must tell you. For as is the case with many stories, there is also some sadness. We wish we did not have to tell you this, but it is part of the story, and share it we must.

**NARRATOR 1:** You see, the hunter had two sisters—two sisters who were very jealous. They were also two very ugly sisters. They were two very ugly and very jealous sisters who would rather hurt people than make them feel good. They would talk and talk about people behind their backs. They were never kind, nor were they ever sweet. They would want nothing more than to hurt others.

**NARRATOR 2:** They would go through the village asking people who the beautiful woman was. Where did she come from? Why had none of her relatives come to the wedding? Why was she always so secretive about her origins? Could it be that she had something to hide?

**SISTER 1:** I do not think she is human. She is much too perfect. Surely she must have a scar. Surely she must have a blemish. She is much too perfect. I do not like her at all!

**SISTER 2:** I agree. Why should she always be happy? There is too much mystery surrounding her. I think she has a secret. I think we need to do something.

**NARRATOR 3:** The two sisters thought and thought, and finally they came up with an evil plan.

**NARRATOR 1:** The two sisters begged their hunter brother to go off and catch some new game. They told him that the wicked money lender was about to throw them out of their house if they did not give him some money. They begged the hunter to go and get some game to sell so that they would not lose their house.

**NARRATOR 2:** They put false tears in their eyes and cried loudly for a long time. They begged their brother to go out into the bush to capture some game. Finally he agreed, and he gathered up his bow and arrows and set out into the forest.

**NARRATOR 3:** A few days after the hunter left, the deer-woman took her basket and headed for the market. The two wicked sisters watched her go and saw their opportunity. They crept up to their brother's house and crawled inside a window. They began searching all over the house.

**SISTER 1:** We have looked in every room. We have looked in every drawer. We have looked in every closet.

**SISTER 2:** We have looked all over this house from the top to the bottom and from side to side. We have looked everywhere. I am very tired . . . . I do not think I can look any more.

**NARRATOR 1:** Just then a small bird fluttered in the rafters of the roof. The two sisters saw the bird and had an idea. They both climbed up into the rafters and soon found the deer skin.

**SISTER 1:** She thinks she is so perfect. Ha!

**SISTER 2:** Wait until we tell all the others about this. Wait until we tell them that this beautiful bride of our brother's is really a deer-woman.

**NARRATOR 2:** Now that the two sisters knew the secret, they went about the town spreading the news everywhere. Everyone was wagging their tongues over the news.

**NARRATOR 3:** The deer-woman heard everyone talking. She heard everyone whispering. The children were making fun of her. Others were calling her names.

**NARRATOR 1:** The deer-woman cried and cried. Finally she could take it no longer. She took down her deer skin from the rafters and slipped it on. Then she walked into the forest, never to return.

**NARRATOR 2:** Soon after, the hunter returned to the village. He called his wife's name, but she was not there. A small bird told him what had happened, and his heart filled with sadness. He knew he had to go into the forest to search for his beloved wife.

**NARRATOR 3:** For seven long years he searched for his wife. He walked to the ends of the earth and back. He looked everywhere for her, but she was nowhere to be found.

**NARRATOR 1:** Finally he decided to walk to the river where he had first seen her. He decided to lie down beside the river and rest for a long time. As he lay sleeping, all the animals of the forest gazed upon him. They took pity on the hunter and decided to help him.

**NARRATOR 2:** The animals searched everywhere. They called everywhere.

**NARRATOR 3:** As the hunter was fast asleep, the bushes beside the river parted and a beautiful deer with a deep bronze skin stepped out. She gazed at the sleeping man with soft eyes and then walked over and nuzzled his face.

**HUNTER:** Who goes there? Oh, it is my long-lost wife. It is my beautiful deer-woman.

**DEER-WOMAN:** Yes, it is I. I have found you and you have found me. My heart is now complete once more.

 From *African Legends, Myths, and Folktales for Readers Theatre* by Anthony D. Fredericks. Westport, CT: Teacher Ideas Press. Copyright © 2008.

**NARRATOR 1:** But that is not quite the end of our story. For we have said that we will tell you the truth, and it is the truth that you must know.

**NARRATOR 2:** Because right there a magical thing happened. The hunter began to shed his human skin. Underneath was a deer—as handsome a creature as you would ever find in the world. He stood next to the deer-woman, nuzzling her neck and sharing his love for her. Together at last, they walked into the woods.

**NARRATOR 3:** And if you are ever in the woods, and if you look very carefully, you may see the deer-woman and the deer-man together. Know that they are forever in love and that they shall never be parted . . . ever again.

From *African Legends, Myths, and Folktales for Readers Theatre* by Anthony D. Fredericks. Westport, CT: Teacher Ideas Press. Copyright © 2008.

The Leopard's Daughter

# The Leopard's Daughter

## (Liberia)

**STAGING:** The two narrators may stand at lecterns or podiums on both sides of the staging area. The other characters should be standing in a random pattern across the staging area. Selected characters (elephant, buffalo, antelope) may wish to perform dancing motions ("Dance of War," "Dance of Peace") as necessary. Each should simulate a spear-throwing motion at the end of the dancing.

---

```
        Leopard      Elephant      Sir Buffalo    Dwarf Antelope
          X             X              X               X
Narrator 1                                                      Narrator 2
  X                                                                 X
```

**NARRATOR 1:** Long ago, in the country of Liberia, there lived a leopard who was king of all the animals. He had many daughters, but there was one daughter who was the most beautiful of all.

**NARRATOR 2:** News of her beauty spread far and wide. All the other animals wanted to marry her because she was so beautiful. But the leopard did not like any of the suitors who came to court his daughter.

**NARRATOR 1:** Finally he decided on a test to decide who would be the best husband for his daughter. So the next day the royal horns and the tribal drums called all the animals of the kingdom together into the middle of a great clearing. And the leopard spoke to them.

**LEOPARD:** Each of you has courted my daughter; each of you wants to be her husband. So I have created a test to see who will be the best husband for her. First, each of you must do the Dance of War to show that you are strong and brave. Then you must do the Dance of Peace to show that there is kindness in your heart. Finally, you must take my royal spear and throw it into the air and count to 10 before it falls to the ground.

**ELEPHANT:** Is that it?

**LEOPARD:** Yes, that is what you must do.

**SIR BUFFALO:** That sounds like an easy test.

**ELEPHANT:** Then I will go first, because I am the biggest and strongest animal in the entire forest.

**NARRATOR 1:** And so the elephant danced the Dance of War to show that he was brave and strong.

[Elephant dances.]

Then he danced the Dance of Peace to show that there was kindness in his heart.

[Elephant dances.]

Finally he took the leopard's spear and threw it up into the air.

[Elephant makes throwing motion.]

But before he could get past the number six, the spear fell to the ground. The elephant failed the test.

**SIR BUFFALO:** Let me try. I am the next strongest animal in the forest.

**NARRATOR 2:** So it was that Sir Buffalo, the next strongest animal in the forest, tried the leopard's test. He danced the Dance of War to show that he was brave.

[Sir Buffalo dances.]

Then he danced the Dance of Peace to show that there was kindness in his heart.

[Sir Buffalo dances.]

Then he took the leopard's spear and threw it into the air.

[Sir Buffalo makes throwing motion.]

From *African Legends, Myths, and Folktales for Readers Theatre* by Anthony D. Fredericks. Westport, CT: Teacher Ideas Press. Copyright © 2008.

But before he could get past the number eight, the spear fell to the ground. The buffalo had failed the test.

**NARRATOR 1:** Then all the other animals tried the test. But all the other animals failed the test. And they were all very angry as they began to walk away.

**ANTELOPE:** Please, let me try.

**NARRATOR 2:** It was then that everyone noticed the dwarf antelope—and they all began to laugh.

[Elephant and buffalo laugh.]

**ELEPHANT:** What makes you think you can do the test?

**BUFFALO:** You are the smallest animal.

**ANTELOPE:** I would like to try.

**LEOPARD:** We must be fair. We must give everyone a chance to do that test.

**NARRATOR 1:** And so the dwarf antelope stepped before all the other animals. He danced the Dance of War to show that he was strong and brave.

[Antelope dances.]

He danced the Dance of Peace to show that there was kindness in his heart.

[Antelope dances.]

Then he took the leopard's spear in his mouth and threw it into the air.

[Antelope makes throwing motion.]

**ANTELOPE:** Five plus five is ten!

**NARRATOR 1:** . . . and the spear clattered to the ground.

**ELEPHANT:** He cheated!

**BUFFALO:** He did not play fair.

**LEOPARD:** No, my friends. All you were asked to do was to count to 10. I did not say HOW you were to make that count.

**NARRATOR 2:** And so it was that the dwarf antelope, the smallest animal in the entire forest, was able to marry the leopard's daughter. And they both lived happily ever after.

**NARRATOR 1:** And the moral to this story is this: We should never judge an individual by how big or how strong he may be, but rather by how he uses his mind.

**NARRATOR 2:** And that is a folktale from the faraway country of Liberia, which is on the great continent of Africa.

From *African Legends, Myths, and Folktales for Readers Theatre* by Anthony D. Fredericks. Westport, CT: Teacher Ideas Press. Copyright © 2008.

Anansi's Fishing Expedition

# Anansi's Fishing Expedition

## (Ghana)

**STAGING:** The two narrators should be seated on tall stools or chairs. The two characters should be standing—holding their scripts in their hands. They may wish to move around the staging area as necessary.

---

| | | | |
|---|---|---|---|
| Narrator 1<br>X | | | Narrator 2<br>X |
| | Anansi<br>X | Onini<br>X | |

**NARRATOR 1:** Anansi was a trickster. Oh, he was a fine boy, but he was a trickster—someone you had to watch out for or he would trick you into doing something you didn't want to. He was a very clever boy indeed.

**NARRATOR 2:** Well, one day Anansi decided that he would like to have some fish. If he had lots of fish, he thought, he could sell some in the marketplace and have some to eat for himself. But catching the fish would take lots of work. He would have to build traps ands set them and check them every day. That would be a lot of work.

**ANANSI:** I know, I will get myself a partner!

**NARRATOR 1:** So Anansi hurried into the village to ask everyone if they would be his partner. Of course, everyone knew about Anansi the trickster. So of course, everyone turned him down.

**NARRATOR 2:** Nobody wanted to go into business with Anansi, because they were sure that they would come out the loser. They knew that they would be cheated by Anansi the trickster.

**NARRATOR 1:** After many people had turned him down, Anansi decided to do something different.

**ANANSI:** What I need is a fool to be my partner.

**NARRATOR 2:** Well, it just so happened that Onini was in the marketplace. He heard Anansi's declaration and walked over to him.

**ONINI:** I have heard that you are looking for a partner to go fishing.

**ANANSI:** That is true. I have a wonderful idea for a business, but I need a partner to make it work. Perhaps you and I could be partners together.

**ONINI:** What would we do as partners, Anansi?

**ANANSI:** We would have a fishing partnership, my friend. A fishing partnership.

**NARRATOR 1:** Everyone tried to warn Onini that Anansi was going to cheat him. But, Onini just smiled and said nothing.

**NARRATOR 2:** The next morning Anansi and Onini went into the forest. They went to a place where there were some nice reeds that were just perfect for building fish traps. Onini took out his knife.

**ONINI:** Because we are partners, we must share the work. I shall begin to cut the reeds for building the traps.

**ANANSI:** What shall I do?

**ONINI:** Why, you shall get tired for me, of course. If I have to cut the reeds, I see no reason why you cannot get tired.

**ANANSI:** What! I do not think that is such a good idea. Why don't you let me cut the reeds, and you can get tired!

From *African Legends, Myths, and Folktales for Readers Theatre* by Anthony D. Fredericks. Westport, CT: Teacher Ideas Press. Copyright © 2008.

**ONINI:** As you wish.

**NARRATOR 1:** Anansi worked all day in the hot sun cutting the reeds. While he was cutting, Onini stretched his arms and rubbed his muscles as if to ease the pain.

**ONINI:** I am very tired from all that work. Now I will carry the reeds to the river and you can have a sore back for me.

**ANANSI:** Oh, no. I will carry the reeds and you shall get the sore back.

**NARRATOR 2:** Anansi carried the reeds down to the river while Onini pretended to have a sore back. He complained and made loud sounds all the way down to the river's edge.

**ANANSI:** Now what?

**ONINI:** Well, we must weave the reeds into traps for the fish. I shall weave the traps and you shall have sore fingers and a sore neck from all the work.

**ANANSI:** Oh, no. This is a partnership. I shall weave the traps and you shall have a sore neck and sore fingers for me.

**ONINI:** Very well, as you wish.

**NARRATOR 1:** The weaving of the traps took a long time. The entire time Anansi kept looking over at Onini, thinking that he was such a fool. Finally the traps were finished and Onini began to collect them.

**ANANSI:** Wait! What are you doing?

**ONINI:** Well, someone has to take the traps out into the water. Since we are partners, I thought I would take them out and set them.

**ANANSI:** Then what shall I do?

**ONINI:** Well, I know that there are many sharks out there. If I get attacked by the shark, then as my partner, you should die for me.

**ANANSI:** Wait a minute! I will take the traps out into the water and set them. Then, if a shark attacks me, you should die.

**NARRATOR 2:** The traps were set in the water, which took a long time. The two partners walked back to the village. Anansi couldn't help looking at his partner. Every now and then, Onini would stop and run his shoulders or rub his arms and groan. Anansi felt very sorry for all the pain his friend was having.

**NARRATOR 1:** The next morning the two partners met once again. It was Anasi who went out to the traps to collect the fish so that he would not have to die if Onini was attacked. There were two large fish in the traps.

**ANANSI:** Let us divide the fish. You shall take one and I shall take one.

**ONINI:** Oh no, my partner. You can have both of these fish. I am sure that there will be more fish tomorrow. You can have these, and I will take the fish we catch tomorrow.

**ANANSI:** I have a better idea. Why don't you take these, and I will take what we get tomorrow?

**ONINI:** Okay, as you wish. I will take these fish.

**NARRATOR 2:** The next morning when the two partners went out to their traps there were four fish.

**ANANSI:** I think you were a fool to take those two fish yesterday. Look at how many fish I have today!

**ONINI:** I am very excited for you. Because that means that I will get all of the fish that we catch tomorrow, and I am sure that there will be many fish tomorrow.

**ANANSI:** Hmmmm. I tell you what, why don't you take these four fish, and I will take the catch tomorrow?

**ONINI:** As you wish, my friend, my partner.

From *African Legends, Myths, and Folktales for Readers Theatre* by Anthony D. Fredericks. Westport, CT: Teacher Ideas Press. Copyright © 2008.

**NARRATOR 1:** The next morning Anansi waded out and collected the traps for the last time. They were beginning to rot and would not hold up for another day of fishing. But when they looked inside the traps there were eight glorious fish inside.

**ANANSI:** Look, my friend, if you had waited one day, all of these fish would have been yours.

**NARRATOR 2:** But, Onini was not looking at the fish. He was looking at the rotted fish traps.

**ONINI:** That is fine. Take your fish. Take them quickly from the traps. I want to get these traps to the market while they are still in fine shape.

**NARRATOR 1:** Anansi looked at the traps. They were falling apart. They were beginning to smell. They were in terrible condition. Anasi was a little suspicious of his friend.

**ANANSI:** What do you mean when you say that these traps are in excellent condition?

**ONINI:** Why, these traps will fetch a handsome price at the market! A very handsome price indeed!

**ANANSI:** Wait a minute! I made those traps myself.

**ONINI:** I know. But I think that if you are going to keep all those fish, the least you can do is let me take the traps.

**ANANSI:** No, no, no. I will keep the traps, and you can keep all the fish.

**NARRATOR 2:** Anansi gathered up all the traps and set off for the market. When he arrived he told everyone of his good fortune and how he had tricked his friend, Onini.

**NARRATOR 1:** But then he tried to sell the rotting traps.

**NARRATOR 2:** Nobody wanted the rotting, smelly traps. Nobody wanted anything to do with them.

**NARRATOR 1:** It was then that Anansi realized that it was he who had been tricked. The trickster had been tricked by an even greater trickster.

**NARRATOR 2:** Soon all the people were laughing at Anansi. Soon all the people were making fun of Anansi.

**NARRATOR 1:** When Onini arrived at the market, everybody cheered. Everybody clapped their hands.

**NARRATOR 2:** [winking at the audience] Oh, Anansi was a trickster, all right. Oh, he was a fine boy, but he was a trickster—someone you had to watch out for or he would trick you into doing something you didn't want to. He was a very clever boy indeed. [wink, wink]

From *African Legends, Myths, and Folktales for Readers Theatre* by Anthony D. Fredericks. Westport, CT: Teacher Ideas Press. Copyright © 2008.

# What Wondrous Powers

## (Togo)

**STAGING:** The three brothers should all be seated on tall stools or chairs. The old man has a small part at the start of the story. After he says his lines, he may exit stage left or stage right. The narrator may be seated or standing at a lectern or podium.

---

| Old Man | Brother 1 | Brother 2 | Brother 3 | |
|---|---|---|---|---|
| X | X | X | X | |
| | | | | Narrator |
| | | | | X |

**NARRATOR:** Many years ago, long before the time when I was born, there was an old man. He had three children, all sons, and one day he called his sons to his bedside.

**OLD MAN:** I am growing old, my sons. I am not as strong as I was in my youth. My strength has gone, and I am unable to provide for my needs. I shall need your help. Please go and obtain for me some food. Please go and obtain for me some clothing. I shall be forever grateful.

**NARRATOR:** And so it was that the three brothers set out across the land. They had traveled for many miles and for many days when, at last, they came to the banks of a swiftly flowing river. With great effort they were able to cross the river, but were very tired when they reached the other side.

**BROTHER 1:** That was a difficult journey.

**BROTHER 2:** Yes, it was. It is good that we are young and strong.

**BROTHER 3:** I do not think that our father would have been able to cross the swift river. He is very old, And he is very weak.

**BROTHER 1:** You are right, brother. But we must not forget our promise to him.

**BROTHER 3:** Yes, indeed. We must do as we were asked.

**BROTHER 2:** So, what shall we do now?

**BROTHER 1:** Well, as the eldest I should make the decision. I believe that it would be best if we separate and go in three different directions.

**BROTHER 3:** Yes, that would be best. By going in three directions we can cover more ground. We will be sure to obtain the food we need. We will be sure to obtain the clothing we need.

**BROTHER 2:** Yes, I agree. It is best if we separate and go in three directions.

**BROTHER 1:** Well, then, brother 3, as the youngest you should take the middle road. Brother 2, as the next oldest, you should take the road to the right. And as the oldest, I will take the road to the left.

**BROTHER 2:** But, what then?

**BROTHER 1:** In a year's time we will meet again, here, at the same spot.

**BROTHER 2:** We will share what we have found.

**BROTHER 3:** And we will return and share it with our father.

**NARRATOR:** And so it was. The three brothers separated. They traveled far. They traveled long. And at the end of a year they all found their way back to the spot beside the swift river.

**BROTHER 1:** [to brother 3] What have you found on your travels?

**BROTHER 3:** I have only found a mirror. But what a magical mirror it is! If you should look into it, you can see all over the country, no matter how far away.

**BROTHER 1:** [to brother 2] What have you found on your travels?

**BROTHER 2:** I have only found a pair of sandals. But what magical sandals they are! They have so much power, that if one puts them on one can walk to any place in the country in just one step.

**BROTHER 3:** [to brother 1] And what have you found, my brother?

**BROTHER 1:** I have found very little, indeed. All I could find was a small calabash of medicine. That is all. But enough talk. Let's look in the mirror and see how our father is.

**NARRATOR:** Brother 3 produced the mirror from his robes, and the three brothers all looked into it. What they saw disturbed them very much. They saw that their father had died, and that the funeral had been held many days previous.

**BROTHER 1:** We must hasten home and see what we can do for our dearly departed father.

**NARRATOR:** Brother 2 brought out the sandals, and all three placed their feet inside. In an instant they were borne to their father's graveside.

**BROTHER 2:** Oh no, our dear father has left this world. We are too late.

**BROTHER 3:** He is gone from us. He is no longer.

**BROTHER 1:** Do not despair, my brothers. Perhaps there is something that can be done.

**NARRATOR:** Brother 1, the eldest, reached into his pocket and produced the calabash of medicine. He gently poured it over the grave. At once the father arose from the grave as though nothing had been wrong with him at all. The three brothers rejoiced and sang. There was a great celebration that night.

[to the audience] But I should ask you a simple question, my friends. Which of the three brothers performed the best? Which of the three brothers had the most wondrous power of all?

# Resources

Legends, myths, and folktales are part of the oral tradition of many cultures. They preserve the stories of the past and heritage of a people. They are often told in informal settings —around campfires, in village ceremonies, or in schools and libraries. Each telling transmits an important part of a culture, an important part of the ancestry of a people.

In each telling, the story changes just a little. The personality of the storyteller, the emphasis on one character over another, the elimination of a scene, or the reaction of a certain audience all shape and influence a story as it is passed from one storyteller to another, from one generation to another. So, too, when stories are eventually transcribed into a written format, they will undergo alterations and modifications. Witness the myriad versions of the Cinderella motif that appear time and again in every culture and every land.

The stories in this collection have come from a wide variety of sources, both written and oral. In some cases I added slight variations in order to make them more "readers theatre friendly." Nevertheless, I have done everything possible to maintain the power, spirit, and magic of each story as it was originally told. For those interested in the original versions (or their related stories), the following sources may be of interest.

Please note that several of the published resources are currently out-of-print and are no longer available through normal book distribution channels. I am particularly indebted to the many librarians and storytellers around the country who helped me track down these stories, folktales, and legends.

## SOURCES OF THE LEGENDS

### Fesito Goes to Market (Uganda)

van Straten, Cicely. *The Great Snake of Kalungu and Other East African Stories*. Pretoria, South Africa: Juventus, 1981.

### The Lion, the Hare, and the Hyena (Kenya)

Savory, Phyllis. *The Little Wise One*. Cape Town, South Africa: Tafelberg, 1990.

### Tiyotiyo (Zimbabwe)

Tiyotiyo (TEE-yo-TEE-yo) is the sound made by small birds as described by the Shona people of eastern Zimbabwe. This folktale is part of the Shona tradition, which celebrates respect for all living things.

### The Hare's Revenge (Zambia)

Savory, Phyllis. *The Little Wise One*. Cape Town, South Africa: Tafelberg, 1990.

### The Enchanting Song of the Magical Bird (Tanzania)

Oelke, Julius. *From the Heart of the Fire*. Cape Town, South Africa: Tafelberg, 1995.

### The Cat Who Came Indoors (Zimbabwe)

Tracey, Hugh. *The Lion on the Path*. New York: Routledge & Kegan Paul, 1967.

### The Boy Who Wanted the Moon (Congo)

Aardema, Verna. *Tales From the Story Hat*. New York: Coward-McCann, 1960.

Finger, Charles Joseph. *Tales from Silver Lands*. Garden City, NY: Doubleday, 1924.

Leach, Maria. *How the People Sang the Mountain Up: How and Why Stories*. New York: Viking, 1967.

### Monkey and Crocodiles (Cameroon)

Matateyou, Emmanuel. *An Anthology of Myths, Legends and Folktales from Cameroon: Storytelling in Africa*. Lewiston, NY: Edwin Mellon Press, 1997.

### The Guardian of the Pool (Central African Republic)

Pitcher, Diana. *Catch Me a River*. Cape Town, South Africa: Tafelberg, 1990.

### Shansa Mutongo Shima (Democratic Republic of the Congo)

Cancel, Robert. *Allegorical Speculation in an Oral Society: The Tabwa Narrative Tradition*. Berkeley: University of California Press, 1989.

Faustin, Charles. *Under the Storyteller's Spell: Folk Tales from the Caribbean*. London: Viking, 1989.

### The Merchant of Tarbooshes (Tunisia)

This story comes from somewhere in Tunisia, but since it is a story from the oral tradition, its sources are difficult to pinpoint. In many traditional tales, one often discovers an unexpected solution to a seemingly insolvable situation. This story is an example of that.

### The Jackal and the Farmer (Algeria)

Frobenius, Leo, and Douglas C. Fox. *African Genesis: Folk Tales and Myths of Africa*. New York: Dover, 1999.

### The Clever Snake Charmer (Morocco)

Albertyn, C. F., and J. F. Spies. *Kinders van die Wêreld*. Cape Town, South Africa: Albertyn, 1963.

### A Most Wise Baker (Egypt)

This story comes from the Egyptian storyteller Eva Dadrian. It is based on actual events and the tradition of breaking bread with family and friends. Breaking bread is a symbol of friendship in many countries, including Egypt.

### The Hare and the Hyena (Botswana)

Savory, Phyllis. *The Little Wise One*. Cape Town, South Africa: Tafelberg, 1990.

### Little Girl and the Monster (Lesotho)

Postma, Minnie. *As Die Maan oor die Lug Loop*. Cape Town, South Africa: Tafelberg, 1986.

### How the Tortoise Won Respect (South Africa)

This story has its origins in the Xhosa people of South Africa. The Xhosa language relies a great deal on natural sounds used in storytelling (some of which were left out of this version).

**Natiki (South Africa)**

Kotzé, Glaudien. *Die Kalbasdraertjie*. Cape Town, South Africa, 1987.

**The Hunter and the Deer-Woman (Nigeria)**

This story was retold by the Nigerian folkteller Funmi Osaba. Her version is based on an ancient Yoruba folktale. The Yoruba occupy much of the southern belt of west Africa and have a storytelling tradition that is thousands of years old.

**The Leopard's Daughter (Liberia)**

Courlander, Harold, George Herzog, and Madye Lee Chastain. *The Cow-Tail Switch and Other West African Stories*. New York: Holt, 1987.

**Anansi's Fishing Expedition (Ghana)**

Appiah, Peggy. *Ananse the Spider: Tales from an Ashanti Village*. New York: Pantheon, 1966.

Arkhurst, Joyce Cooper. *The Adventures of Spider: West African Folktales*. Boston: Little, Brown, 1964.

**What Wondrous Powers (Togo)**

Abrahams, Roger D. *African Folktales*. New York; Pantheon, 1983.

Cardinall, A. W. *Tales Told in Togoland*. Oxford: Oxford University Press, 1931.

# READERS THEATRE BOOKS

Barchers, S. *Fifty Fabulous Fables: Beginning Readers Theatre*. Westport, CT: Teacher Ideas Press, 1997.

———. *From Atalanta to Zeus*. Westport, CT: Teacher Ideas Press, 2001.

———. *Judge for Yourself*. Westport, CT: Teacher Ideas Press, 2004.

———. *Multicultural Folktales: Readers Theatre for Elementary Students*. Westport, CT: Teacher Ideas Press, 2000.

———. *Readers Theatre for Beginning Readers*. Westport, CT: Teacher Ideas Press, 1993.

———. *Scary Readers Theatre*. Westport, CT: Teachers Ideas Press, 1994.

Barchers, S., and C. R. Pfeffinger. *More Readers Theatre for Beginning Readers*. Westport, CT: Teacher Ideas Press, 2006.

Barchers, S., and J. L. Kroll. *Classic Readers Theatre for Young Adults*. Westport, CT: Teacher Ideas Press, 2002.

Barnes, J. W. *Sea Songs*. Westport, CT: Teacher Ideas Press, 2004.

Black, A. N. *Born Storytellers*. Westport, CT: Teacher Ideas Press, 2005.

Criscoe, B. L., and P. J. Lanasa. *Fairy Tales for Two Readers*. Westport, CT: Teacher Ideas Press, 1995.

Dixon, N., A. Davies, and C. Politano. *Learning with Readers Theatre: Building Connections*. Winnipeg, MB: Peguis Publishers, 1996.

Fredericks, A. D. *Frantic Frogs and Other Frankly Fractured Folktales for Readers Theatre*. Westport, CT: Teacher Ideas Press, 1993.

————. *MORE Frantic Frogs and Other Frankly Fractured Folktales for Readers Theatre.* Westport, CT: Teacher Ideas Press, 2008.

————. *Mother Goose Readers Theatre for Beginning Readers.* Westport, CT: Teacher Ideas Press, 2007.

————. *Nonfiction Readers Theatre for Beginning Readers.* Westport, CT: Teacher Ideas Press, 2007.

————. *Readers Theatre for American History.* Westport, CT: Teacher Ideas Press, 2001.

————. *Science Fiction Readers Theatre.* Westport, CT: Teacher Ideas Press, 2002.

————. *Silly Salamanders and Other Slightly Stupid Stories for Readers Theatre.* Westport, CT: Teacher Ideas Press, 2000.

————. *Songs and Rhymes Readers Theatre for Beginning Readers.* Westport, CT: Teacher Ideas Press, 2008.

————. *Tadpole Tales and Other Totally Terrific Treats for Readers Theatre.* Westport, CT: Teacher Ideas Press, 1997.

Garner, J. *Wings of Fancy: Using Readers Theatre to Study Fantasy Genre.* Westport, CT: Teacher Ideas Press, 2006

Georges, C., and C. Cornett. *Reader's Theatre.* Buffalo, NY: D.O.K. Publishers, 1990.

Haven, K. *Great Moments in Science: Experiments and Readers Theatre.* Westport, CT: Teacher Ideas Press, 1996.

Jenkins, D. R. *Just Deal with It.* Westport, CT: Teacher Ideas Press, 2004.

Johnson, T. D., and D. R. Louis. *Bringing it All Together: A Program for Literacy.* Portsmouth, NH: Heinemann, 1990.

Kroll, J. L. *Simply Shakespeare.* Westport, CT: Teacher Ideas Press, 2003.

Latrobe, K. H., C. Casey, and L. A. Gann. *Social Studies Readers Theatre for Young Adults.* Westport, CT: Teacher Ideas Press, 1991.

Laughlin, M. K., P. T. Black, and K. H. Latrobe. *Social Studies Readers Theatre for Children.* Westport, CT: Teacher Ideas Press, 1991.

————. *Readers Theatre for Children.* Westport, CT: Teacher Ideas Press, 1990.

Martin, J. M. *12 Fabulously Funny Fairy Tale Plays.* New York: Instructor Books, 2002.

Peterson, C. *Around the World Through Holidays.* Westport, CT: Teacher Ideas Press, 2005.

Pfeffinger, C. R. *Character Counts.* Westport, CT: Teacher Ideas Press, 2003.

————. *Holiday Readers Theatre.* Westport, CT: Teacher Ideas Press, 1994.

Pugliano-Martin, C. *25 Just-Right Plays for Emergent Readers (grades K–1).* New York: Scholastic, 1999.

Shepard, A. *Folktales on Stage: Children's Plays for Readers Theatre.* Olympia, WA: Shepard Publications, 2003.

————. *Readers on Stage: Resources for Readers Theatre.* Olympia, WA: Shepard Publications, 2004.

————. *Stories on Stage: Children's Plays for Readers Theatre.* Olympia, WA: Shepard Publications, 2005.

Sloyer, S. *From the Page to the Stage.* Westport, CT: Teacher Ideas Press, 2003.

Smith, C. *Extraordinary Women from U.S. History*. Westport, CT: Teacher Ideas Press, 2003.

Wolf, J. M. *Cinderella Outgrows the Glass Slipper and Other Zany Fractured Fairy Tale Plays*. New York: Scholastic, 2002.

Wolfman, J. *How and Why Stories for Readers Theatre*. Westport, CT: Teacher Ideas Press, 2004.

Worthy, J. *Readers Theatre for Building Fluency: Strategies and Scripts for Making the Most of This Highly Effective, Motivating, and Research-Based Approach to Oral Reading*. New York: Scholastic, 2005.

# WEB SITES

http://www.aaronshep.com/rt/RTE.html
How to use readers theatre, sample scripts from a children's author who specializes in readers theatre, and an extensive list of resources.

http://www.cdli.ca/CITE/langrt.htm
This site has lots of information, including "What is Readers Theatre," "Readers Theatre Scripts," "Writing Scripts," "Recommended Print Resources," and "Recommended On-line Resources."

http://www.teachingheart.net/readerstheater.htm
Here you discover lots of plays and scripts to print and read in your classroom or library.

http://literacyconnections.com/readerstheater
There is an incredible number of resources and scripts at this all-inclusive site.

http://www.proteacher.com/070173.shmtl
This site is a growing collection of tens of thousands of ideas shared by teachers across the United States and around the world.

http://www.readerstheatredigest.com
This is an online magazine of ideas, scripts, and teaching strategies.

http://www.readerstheatre.escd.net
This site has more than 150 short poems, stories, and chants for readers theatre.

http://www.storycart.com
Storycart Press's subscription service provides an inexpensive opportunity to have timely scripts delivered to teachers or librarians each month. Each script is created or adapted by well-known writer Suzanne Barchers, author of several readers theatre books (see above).

# PROFESSIONAL ORGANIZATION

Institute for Readers Theatre
P.O. Box 421262
San Diego, CA 92142
(858) 277-4274
http://www.readerstheatreinstitute.com

# More Teacher and Librarian Resources

by

## Anthony D. Fredericks

The following books are available from Teacher Ideas Press (88 Post Road West, Westport, CT 06881); 1-800-225-5800; http://www.teacherideaspress.com.

***Frantic Frogs and Other Frankly Fractured Folktales for Readers Theatre.*** ISBN 1-56308-174-1. (124pp.; $19.50).

Have you heard "Don't Kiss Sleeping Beauty, She's Got Really Bad Breath" or "The Brussels Sprouts Man (The Gingerbread Man's Unbelievably Strange Cousin)"? This resource (grades 4–8) offers 30 reproducible satirical scripts for rip-roaring dramatics in any classroom or library.

***The Integrated Curriculum: Books for Reluctant Readers, Grades 2-5.*** 2nd ed. ISBN 0-87287-994-1. (220pp.; $22.50).

This book presents guidelines for motivating and using literature with reluctant readers. It contains more than 40 book units on titles carefully selected to motivate the most reluctant readers.

***Investigating Natural Disasters Through Children's Literature: An Integrated Approach.*** ISBN 1-56308-861-4. (193pp.; $28.00).

Tap into students' inherent awe of storms, volcanic eruptions, hurricanes, earthquakes, tornadoes, floods, avalanches, landslides, and tsunamis to open their minds to the wonders and power of the natural world. .

***Involving Parents Through Children's Literature: P–K.*** ISBN 1-56308-022-2. (86 pp.; $15.00).

***Involving Parents Through Children's Literature: Grades 1–2.*** ISBN 1-56308-012-5. (96pp.; $14.50).

***Involving Parents Through Children's Literature: Grades 3–4.*** ISBN 1-56308-013-3. (96pp.; $15.50).

***Involving Parents Through Children's Literature: Grades 5–6.*** ISBN 1-56308-014-1. (108pp.; $16.00).

This series of four books offers engaging activities for adults and children that stimulate comprehension and promote reading enjoyment. Reproducible activity sheets based on high-quality children's books are designed in a convenient format so that children can take them home.

***The Librarian's Complete Guide to Involving Parents Through Children's Literature: Grades K–6.*** ISBN 1-56308-538-0. (138pp.; $24.50).

Activities for 101 children's books are presented in a reproducible format, so librarians can distribute them to students to take home and share with parents.

***MORE Frantic Frogs and Other Frankly Fractured Folktales for Readers Theatre.*** ISBN 978-1-59158-628-9. (166pp.; $25.00).

Remember all the fun you had with the original *Frantic Frogs*? Well, they're back!! Here's another laugh-fest overflowing with scripts that will leave students (and teachers) rolling in the aisles (Don't miss "The Original Hip-Hop (by Busta Frog)") .

***More Social Studies Through Children's Literature: An Integrated Approach.*** ISBN 1-56308-761-8. (226pp.; $27.50).

Energize your social studies curriculum with dynamic, hands-on, minds-on projects based on such great children's books as *Amazing Grace*, *Fly Away Home*, and *Lon Po Po*. This book is filled with an array of activities and projects sure to "energize" any social studies curriculum.

***Mother Goose Readers Theatre for Beginning Readers.*** ISBN 978-1-59158-500-8. (168pp.; $25.00).

Designed especially for educators in the primary grades, this resource provides engaging opportunities that capitalize on children's enjoyment of Mother Goose rhymes. There is lots to share and lots to enjoy in the pages of this resource.

***Much More Social Studies Through Children's Literature: A Collaborative Approach.*** ISBN 978-1-59158-445-2. (278pp.; $35.00).

This collection of dynamic, literature-based activities will help any teacher or librarian energize the entire social studies curriculum and implement national (and state) standards. This resource is filled with hundreds of hands-on, minds-on projects.

***Nonfiction Readers Theatre for Beginning Readers.*** ISBN 978-1-59158-499-5. (220pp.; $25.00).

This collection of science and social studies nonfiction scripts for beginning readers is sure to "jazz up" any language arts program in grades 1–3. Teachers and librarians will discover a wealth of creative opportunities to enhance fluency, comprehension, and appreciation of nonfiction literature.

***Readers Theatre for American History.*** ISBN 1-56308-860-6. (174pp.; $30.00).

This book offers a participatory approach to American history in which students become active in several historical events. These 24 scripts give students a "you are there" perspective on critical milestones and colorful moments that have shaped the American experience.

***Science Adventures with Children's Literature:*** A Thematic Approach. ISBN 1-56308-417-1. (190pp.; $24.50).

Focusing on the *National Science Education Standards,* this activity-centered resource uses a wide variety of children's literature to integrate science across the elementary curriculum. With a thematic approach, it features the best in science trade books along with stimulating hands-on, minds on activities in all the sciences.

***Science Discoveries on the Net: An Integrated Approach.*** ISBN 1-56308-823-1. (316pp.; $27.50).

> This book is designed to help teachers integrate the Internet into their science programs and enhance the scientific discoveries of students. The 88 units emphasize key concepts—based on national and state standards—throughout the science curriculum.

***Silly Salamanders and Other Slightly Stupid Stuff for Readers Theatre.*** ISBN 1-56308-825-8. (162pp.; $23.50).

> The third entry in the "wild and wacky" readers theatre trilogy is just as crazy and weird as the first two. This unbelievable resource offers students in grades 3–6 dozens of silly send-ups of well-known fairy tales, legends, and original stories.

***Social Studies Discoveries on the Net: An Integrated Approach.*** ISBN 1-56308-824-X. (276pp.; $26.00).

> This book is designed to help teachers integrate the Internet into their social studies programs and enhance the classroom discoveries of students. The 75 units emphasize key concepts—based on national and state standards—throughout the social studies curriculum.

***Social Studies Through Children's Literature: An Integrated Approach***. ISBN 1-87287-970-4. (192pp.; $24.00).

> Each of the 32 instructional units contained in this resource utilizes an activity-centered approach to elementary social studies, featuring children's picture books such as *Ox-Cart Man, In Coal Country,* and *Jambo Means Hello.*

***Songs and Rhymes Readers Theatre for Beginning Readers.*** ISBN 978-1-59158-627-2. (178pp.; $25.00).

> Bring music, song, and dance into your classroom language arts curriculum with this delightful collection of popular rhymes and ditties. Beginning readers will enjoy learning about familiar characters through this engaging collection of scripts.

***Tadpole Tales and Other Totally Terrific Titles for Readers Theatre.*** ISBN 1-56308-547-X. (116pp.; $18.50).

> A follow-up volume to the best-selling *Frantic Frogs and Other Frankly Fractured Folktales for Readers Theatre*, this book provides primary level readers (grades 1–4) with a humorous assortment of wacky tales based on well-known Mother Goose rhymes. More than 30 scripts and dozens of extensions will keep students rolling in the aisles.

# Index

# About the Author and Illustrator

**Anthony D. Fredericks** (afredericks60@comcast.net). Tony's background includes more than 37 years of experience as a classroom teacher, reading specialist, curriculum coordinator, staff developer, professional storyteller, and college professor. He is a prolific author, having written more than 65 teacher resource books, including the enormously popular *More Frantic Frogs and Other Frankly Fractured Folktales for Readers Theatre*, the best-selling *Guided Reading in Grades 3–6*, the celebrated *Much More Social Studies Through Children's Literature*, and the dynamic *Readers Theatre for American History*.

In addition, he has authored more than three dozen award-winning children's books, including *The Tsunami Quilt: Grandfather's Story, Near One Cattail: Turtles, Logs and Leaping Frogs, Dinosaur Droppings, Animal Sharpshooters*, and *A Is for Anaconda: A Rainforest Alphabet Book*.

Tony currently teaches elementary methods courses in reading, language arts, science, social studies, and children's literature at York College in York, Pennsylvania. He is also a popular and enthusiastic visiting children's author at elementary schools throughout North America, where he celebrates books, writing, and storytelling.

**Bongaman** (nkbongaman@yahoo.com) was born in Jakiri in the Northwest Province of Cameroon. His family later moved to Kumbo and eventually to Bamenda, where they still live today. Educated at several Catholic schools, he obtained his ordinary and advanced level certificates.

Bongaman studied under two of Cameroon's leading artists, Yeman Emmanuel and Nzante Spee. After two years of study at the Nzante Spee Academy of Fine Art, he moved to Yaounde, the national capital of Cameroon. There he opened his own successful gallery, selling hundreds of paintings to collectors from around the world. He also had several one-man exhibitions organized by the French Cultural Center in Cameroon. In addition, he has won many artistic awards from the Spanish Embassy, UNESCO, and the Cameroon Cultural Center, among others. In 2005 he was recognized for his artistic skills by the president of the republic and the National Museum of Cameroon.

In January 2007 Bongaman emigrated to the United States. He and his wife, Cassie, now live outside Washington, D.C. In addition to working for a metal artist in Maryland, he continues to paint and display his artistic talents.